THE REFERENCE SHELF   VOLUME 34 NUMBER 2

SOUTH AFRICA

EDITED BY GRANT S. McCLELLAN

THE H. W. WILSON COMPANY

NEW YORK   1962

THE REFERENCE SHELF

Copyright © 1962
By The H. W. Wilson Company
Library of Congress Catalog Card No. 62-9026

PRINTED IN THE UNITED STATES OF AMERICA

PREFACE

Riots, treason trials, police atrocities, and predictions of violent explosion have punctuated the news from South Africa for more than a decade. During this period the Republic of South Africa, formerly the Union of South Africa, has been ruled by the Nationalist party, which gains its greatest support from the dominant Afrikaner white population. But perhaps the majority of the English-speaking white population has views similar to those of the Nationalists.

These views have become symbolized throughout the world as the policy of *apartheid* (pronounced a-PART-hate)—the official policy of the present government. That regime has been called a paradox—a parliamentary government for the three million whites, ruling as a virtual police state over some eleven million nonwhites. South Africa is a multiracial society in which integration of its various races has proceeded, at least in the economic realm, to a degree which most whites either ignore or would like to reverse.

At present, most government efforts are directed toward dis-allowing all efforts toward integration or even interracial consultation to take place. It is this factor, the virtual breakdown of communications among the races in South Africa, which forebodes disaster. Significantly, the articles in this book suggest almost no ways in which much consultation can soon again become possible. And yet many persons of all races in South Africa and among South Africa's friends abroad passionately hope that a new beginning can be made.

It is characteristic of many different views of South Africa that passion and hope run deep. And within South Africa these feelings are inextricably bound up with patriotism. Both the whites and Africans feel deeply about their country and for sound historical reasons neither group has yet flatly denied "its" country to the other group. But that may come. There is much hate in this troubled land; there is much fear too. All of the conditions for violent explosion seem at hand.

South Africa has become an international problem also; and here too are extremes of passion and hope. All Africa is now on the march and the repercussions of the Africans' advance toward freedom in other parts of the continent will not wait on official Nationalist policies. The Western world is more and more involved with regard to South Africa's course. If racial war occurs, the West will perforce take action. For what purposes? On this score, as this compilation shows, there has been little firm thinking.

Because recent events have moved so rapidly in South Africa, certain of the articles included here are dated in terminology. Thus, references to the Union of South Africa occur, though the Republic came into being at the end of May 1961. Representative comments on South Africa's problems, both from the Republic and abroad, written before that date are no less valid than those written later.

All discussion about South Africa is shot through with concern for *apartheid;* the reader will soon discover why. Background articles are included which place the present period in perspective. Nor is the situation wholly "either-or," either chaos or progress toward full freedom for all races in South Africa. Many forces and diverse opinions are at work in South Africa. These also are represented in this collection.

The editor wishes to thank the various authors and publishers who have granted permission for the use of materials included in this book.

GRANT S. McCLELLAN

February 1962

CONTENTS

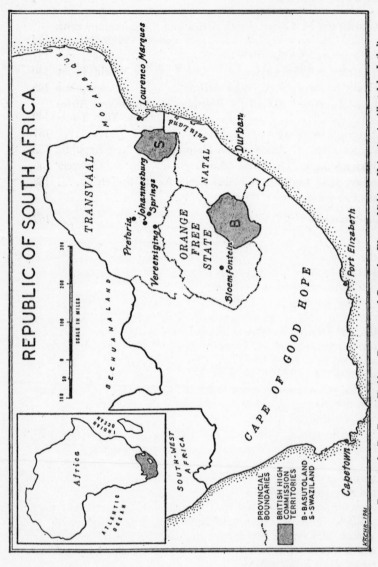

REPUBLIC OF SOUTH AFRICA

MOÇAMBIQUE

Lourenco Marques

TRANSVAAL

Pretoria
Johannesburg
Springs
Vereeniging

Zululand

S

Durban

NATAL

ORANGE
FREE
STATE

B

Bloemfontein

BECHUANALAND

SCALE IN MILES

100   50   0   100   200   300

CAPE OF GOOD HOPE

Port Elizabeth

Capetown

KRCHR-1961

INDIAN OCEAN

Africa

SOUTH-WEST
AFRICA

ATLANTIC
OCEAN

——— PROVINCIAL
BOUNDARIES

BRITISH HIGH
COMMISSION
TERRITORIES

B-BASUTOLAND
S-SWAZILAND

From map by Dr. Eugene Kirchherr, Department of Geography, Western Michigan University, in *Albert John Luthuli and the South African Race Conflict*, by Edward Callan. Western Michigan University Press, Kalamazoo. '62. p 8. Copyright 1962 by the Institute of Regional Studies, Western Michigan University. Reprinted by permission.

I. LAND OF TROUBLE AND WEALTH

EDITOR'S INTRODUCTION

South Africa has long been a land of conflict. Almost at the same time that colonists from Europe were coming to America, three hundred years ago, the ancestors of both whites and Africans in South Africa were invading that land. Since then conflict has persisted, and there have also been hostilities between the two white groups—Dutch and English—now called Afrikaners and English-speaking whites. By the time the Dutch and English clashed, the wealth of empire was at stake.

Conflict remains and so does wealth, long symbolized by the diamonds of South Africa. Part of the story is told in this section in a swift look at the history and present state of the South African economy.

The section opens with a brief note on the confusing racial situation, with information about recent events in South Africa that are referred to throughout the text. A *Life* magazine article reviews the history of South Africa, and this is followed by a selection in which a noted South African historian, Leo Marquard, sketches the picture today with the advent of the new Republic. Anthony Sampson, a South African correspondent for the London *Observer,* tells about the Africans and their life in the industrial centers.

South Africa is shown in economic perspective by John Hughes, a staff correspondent of the *Christian Science Monitor;* his article is followed by an account drawn from *Fortune* magazine of the truly fabulous world of the diamond and mining industry in South Africa. Then a note on the present economic crisis which in part results from the government's apartheid policies. The section ends with a wide-ranging comment by Vernon McKay, an American exchange professor to South Africa, which deals with recent events and introduces a number of topics dealt with more fully in later sections of the book.

THE LAND AND THE PEOPLE [1]

The Union of South Africa is composed of four provinces—Cape, Natal, Transvaal and Orange Free State, with a total area of 472,359 square miles. Within its geographical boundaries is the protectorate of Basutoland, which is controlled by a resident commissioner under the direction of the high commissioner for the United Kingdom, who also administers the contiguous territorial protectorates of Bechuanaland and Swaziland. Adjacent to the Union of South Africa is the territory of South-West Africa over which the former was granted a . . . mandate under Article 22 of the Covenant of the League of Nations, December 17, 1920. [See "South-West Africa," "A Call for Elections in South-West Africa," and "African States Protest," in Section IV, below.]

At the time of the last census, May 8, 1951, the total population of the Union of South Africa was 12,646,375, and of this number the official racial classification was as follows: "European" 2,642,713; "African" 8,535,341; "Coloured" 1,103,405, and "Asian" 366,644. . . . The term "European" applies to all whites as defined by South African law. (Conversely, "nonwhite" applies to all non-"Europeans.") Further the white group can be generally divided between "Afrikaners," which includes those whose first or mother tongue is Afrikaans and who are primarily of Dutch descent (some also of Huguenot and German stock), and the English-speaking, primarily British, element. The "African" classified by law to be "any person who is generally accepted as a member of any aboriginal race or tribe of Africa," is also referred to as "native," "Kaffir" (derogatory), or, less precisely, "Bantu." The "Coloureds" are those who are neither Africans nor Asians nor whites. The "Asians" include Indians and other Asiatic groups. Also in current usage are the terms "blacks" and "nonwhites." The latter is a convenient comprehensive reference to Africans, Coloureds and Indians.

The present government of the Union of South Africa is that of the Nationalist party under the leadership of Dr. H. F. Verwoerd. . . . The Nationalist party, which draws its support mainly from the Afrikaner rural population, came into power in 1948 with a majority of the House of Assembly of the bicameral

[1] From *South Africa and the Rule of Law*, by the International Commission of Jurists. Geneva, Switzerland. '60. p 11-13.

parliament. At that time Dr. D. F. Malan succeeded Field Marshal J. C. Smuts as premier. Field Marshal Smuts had held that position since 1939 as head of the United party. The Nationalist party platform and the expressed policy of the government is one of apartheid which, in brief, aims towards the separate development of the nonwhite ethnic groups. This concept cannot, however, be uniquely attributed to the present government or recent times. . . . Indeed discriminatory provisions can be found throughout the legislative history, and as early as 1917 Smuts is quoted as saying that confusion arising from mixing black and white, with the result that the black would be lifted up to degrade the white, could only be prevented by keeping white and black apart. . . .

Recent events of interest . . . are the treason trial, the Sharpeville shootings, and the declaration of the emergency. The treason trial, commencing in 1956 with the arrest of 156 persons on charges of treason, resulted in prolonged detention of the accused, the last of the detainees being released on August 31, 1960, and [has only recently been concluded. See "A Trial and Its Meaning," in Section III, below.] The Sharpeville shootings which occurred March 21, 1960, involved police firing on crowds demonstrating against the pass laws requiring that all Africans carry and present upon demand a document of identification. Finally, on March 30, 1960, a state of emergency was proclaimed by the government for eighty districts of the Union of South Africa. The emergency . . . ended on August 31, 1960. [See "South Africa Faces the Future," in Section III, below.]

HISTORY'S BEQUEST [2]

The rulers of the Union of South Africa are 1.8 million whites who call themselves Afrikaners and are outnumbered $5\frac{1}{2}$ to 1 by the blacks they dominate. The descendants of Dutch and French Huguenot settlers, they speak their own version of Dutch called Afrikaans and are probably the most parochial white people anywhere.

The country they govern is a bush and tableland chunk of geography about the size of Germany, France and Italy combined.

[2] From "South Africa Torn by Fury," by Gene Farmer, foreign news editor of *Life*. *Life*. 48:34-7. Ap. 11, '60. Courtesy *Life* Magazine. Copyright 1960 Time Inc.

It produces 43 per cent of the world's gold, about half again as much gold as the United States and Soviet Russia put together. Along with the Afrikaners, its 14.6 million inhabitants include an estimated 9.7 million native blacks; a half million Indians; 1.4 million Coloureds, who are a mixture of Malay, African and white; and 1.2 million English-speaking Europeans.

The Afrikaner minority has run South Africa politically for the past decade through the Nationalist party and a secret society called the *Broederbond,* a Ku Klux Klan-like organization which . . . is almost as anti-Freemason, anti-Catholic and anti-Jewish as it is antinative. During the 1950's the policy of apartheid . . . has been imposed so implacably on natives, Coloureds and Indians that the minds of this nation's rulers seem, to an American, almost demented. The reasons for this attitude are deeply rooted in the Union's peculiar three-hundred-year history.

The British planted the Union Jack in 1620 in what is now Cape Town, but they did not stay. The first permanent settlement there was founded in 1652 by a Dutch surgeon named Jan van Riebeeck. He intended it only as a victualing post for ships of the Dutch East India Company and no immediate attempt was made to colonize the country. The colony grew slowly and in 1685 the Dutch settlers were joined by some two hundred Huguenots who fled . . . [from persecution in France]. The British occupied Cape Colony during the Napoleonic wars to secure their sea communications, taking title by the Convention of London in 1814. In the 1820's Britons started emigrating to the Cape in numbers, and in 1843 a second colony, the Natal, was annexed by the British.

The British did not get on with the Dutch. There were acute differences in language, temperament and, most importantly, religion. The Dutch settlers were Calvinist and fiercely fundamentalist; the British were Anglican. Already, in the view of the Dutch, the British were "too liberal" in their attitude toward the natives. Here began an ever-widening schism which plagues South Africa's European population to this day.

The schism was permanently confirmed in 1836 when, to get away from the British, some twelve thousand Dutch-Huguenots loaded their ox wagons and shoved off northward, herding their cattle and sheep before them, into a vast uncharted region thinly populated by Bushmen and Hottentots. This was "The

Great Trek," the single most important event in South African history. Although only 25 per cent of the Dutch-Huguenots in the Cape were involved, their adventure conveys to the Afrikaner today, as John Gunther [the well-known journalist and author of *Inside Africa*] has remarked, "what Paul Revere's Ride, Custer's Last Stand, Valley Forge, and the Alamo all convey to Americans."

Coincidentally, a great southward migration of the black Bantu tribes from the equatorial areas of Central Africa was just picking up steam. To this day the Afrikaner defends his privileged position in South Africa on the grounds that his ancestors got there first. For all practical purposes the race ended in a tie with the natives.

In spite of drought, the rinderpest disease which killed their cattle and the belligerent Zulus, the *Voortrekkers* won the territory. Andries Pretorius, for whose family the Union's administrative capital of Pretoria was later named, smashed the Zulus in the Battle of Blood River in 1838. Some of the trekkers dropped off in what later became the Orange Free State, where the British outpost commander was only too glad to let them settle on his Godforsaken acres. Others pushed as far north as the town of Louis Trichardt, 245 miles north of Johannesburg, and as far east as Volksrust, near the Transvaal-Natal border.

It was an epic feat, particularly for the *Voortrekker* women, whose fortitude and endurance is part of the Afrikaner legend. But it had the effect of isolating an impoverished and instinctively insular people. Even at this early date they had rather definite ideas about how to deal with the African native, and the trek cut them off from Europe's nineteenth-century liberal enlightenment. They had very few doctors and teachers. Their diet featured biltong, the same jerked meat American pioneer trappers ate, and milk tart, still prepared by Afrikaner housewives for very special afternoon teas. Their children's education consisted mainly of a Calvinistic and literal interpretation of the Bible, emphasizing an ancient curse: "Let them be hewers of wood and drawers of water."

Their language took shape, first as slang, then as vernacular. It was corruption of Dutch, and it was originally called "kitchen Dutch" because it was invented for the benefit of the native kitchen boy who could not wrap his tongue around proper Dutch.

The people called themselves Afrikaners, or Boers, "boer" being an Afrikaans word for "farmer." This language, now the mother tongue of 60 per cent of South Africa's white population, is something of which the Afrikaners are irrationally proud, even though they did not officially begin to codify it in dictionary form until 1925. Its vocabulary is woefully limited and new words have to be invented all the time. Faced with the problem of how to . . . [translate] "motor scooter" into Afrikaans, the government dictionary staff came up with *bromponie,* which combined *brom* (to buzz like a bee) and *ponie* (a miniature horse or pony).

In the 1850's the Boers formed two independent republics— the Orange Free State and the South African Republic, later known as the Transvaal. Nobody cared; these people seemed to have nothing the world could possibly covet. This was soon to change.

In 1867 diamonds were discovered on the Orange River. This brought a flock of *uitlanders,* or foreigners, into the picture. Mostly they were British; indeed the British went so far as to annex the Transvaal Republic in 1877, but after the Boers revolted a Liberal Gladstone government [in Britain] let it go again. Then, in 1886, a dead-busted British diamond prospector named George Harrison discovered that the craggy Witwatersrand ("Ridge of White Waters") towering over Johannesburg was literally a mountain of gold. Harrison died busted, but he changed the course of history.

Britons and British capital poured in, both organized by that fantastic genius Cecil Rhodes. He organized De Beers Consolidated Mines Ltd., the greatest mining combine the world had ever seen, taking the name from a Dutch farmer on whose land an early strike was made. The wealth at stake was immense. One farm that sold for twelve oxen in the 1880's has since produced £75 million in gold.

The coffers of the Transvaal Republic just bulged with gold, but its dour president, "Oom Paul" ("Uncle Paul") Kruger, one of the most remarkable men ever born in Africa, feared and resented these outside influences. So did the other Boers. The British were good merchants; they understood money matters and things like insurance. Kruger was a stovepipe-hatted Calvinist who had sixteen children by three wives and firmly believed the world was flat. He made citizenship difficult for foreigners and raised taxes on their earnings from the gold fields.

In 1895 a friend of Rhodes, Sir Leander Starr Jameson, organized the famous "Jameson Raid" into the Transvaal to overthrow Kruger. The foreigners were then supposed to arise— but they did not. Rhodes, who had become prime minister of the Cape Colony, was ruined politically and had to resign. But war between the British and the Boers was by then inevitable.

It broke out in 1899 and lasted three years, attracting the presence, among others, of such martial types as the late Will Rogers, W. C. Fields and cowboy actor Tom Mix. When asked at the time what side he was on, Mix replied, "Either side. I haven't had a chance to check up on what they're fighting about." The British won the war, but not without having to learn once again certain lessons about bush fighting which the American Indians taught General Braddock's men in 1755. The Orange Free State and the Transvaal disappeared and what is now the Union of South Africa came under British rule. Rhodes died while the war was still going on. The war made another Englishman famous. Winston Churchill was captured by the Boers as a war correspondent, escaped and made his way back to London a celebrity.

The British smashed Afrikaner sovereignty, for the time being. But they made a generous peace with the Boers. The two principal Boer military commanders, General Louis Botha and General Jan Christiaan Smuts, cooperated with the British on the basis of let-bygones-be-bygones. But simultaneously another general, Barry Hertzog, was busy laying the foundations for present-day Afrikaner nationalism. Hertzog, who later served fifteen years as prime minister, was one of the leaders of the drive which won South African autonomy in 1910. The Afrikaners also won equal status for the Dutch language with English. (At that time Afrikaans was still sixteen years away from being formalized.)

By this time another racial group had entered the picture: the Indians, brought in originally by the British to work the sugar and tea plantations. In 1897, however, legislation was enacted in Natal to check the entry of "free" Indians and their ubiquitous trading activities. Earlier in the same year a twenty-seven-year-old Indian lawyer named Mohandas Gandhi, leading a passive resistance fight for equality, had to be rescued from a Durban mob by the police. Since 1913 Indians have been forbidden to enter the Union as immigrants. The Indians now own one third of the land in the Durban metropolitan area. They have not assimilated. . . . The Indians remain a formidable economic force all over East and South Africa, like the Chinese in southeast Asia, and they are disliked accordingly. . . .

Between 1910 and the end of World War II, the man who preserved political equilibrium in South Africa was *"Slim* Jannie" Smuts *(slim* is an Afrikaner word meaning "crafty"). He became Winston Churchill's great friend and took the Union on Britain's side into both world wars. In the process he made political combinations as the occasion demanded. He was not an apostle of apartheid; he was too much an intellectual to hate the blacks. But in effect he practiced apartheid.

When Smuts by sheer force of personality brought South Africa into World War II, many Afrikaners accused him of fighting Britain's war. Among the objectors were Dr. Daniel Malan, Johannes Strijdom and Dr. Hendrik Verwoerd. All three followed Smuts, in that order, as Union prime ministers.

Malan made it as a result of the 1948 election, which the Nationalist party won on a violently antinative platform. He was a moderate, though, compared to his successors. Malan was replaced in 1954 by Strijdom, a onetime ostrich farmer. . . . Strijdom's taking over was a tremendously significant event because he was a *Broederbonder.*

The *Broederbond* ("Band of Brothers"), which is supposed to have been founded as an anti-British instrument in World War I, probably numbers about four thousand members—nobody knows for sure. *Broederbonders* include an astonishing percentage of teachers and Dutch Reformed ministers, almost certainly a majority of the present cabinet, and most particularly Dr. Verwoerd, who became prime minister . . . [in September 1958] after Strijdom's death. A kindly-looking fifty-eight-year-old Father Christmas type with a ruddy face and a cherubic smile, Verwoerd was pro-German during the last war. . . .

He is ruthlessly logical. Indeed he may be the only man in the whole country who knows what the practical application of apartheid will cost and who believes in it anyway. Verwoerd advocates something going beyond apartheid—what the Afrikaners call *baaskap,* or out-and-out mastership. Most of the really restrictive legislation on this subject has in the past decade been passed by the Malan and Strijdom governments in which Verwoerd was minister of native affairs. Now, as prime minister, Verwoerd is riding his own tiger.

Verwoerd's basic idea is to create a number of *Bantustans* in which natives will live to themselves, removed from white society. Eventually they will have some kind of self-government within their own compounds. Conceivably this could work, but there are two immense practical difficulties—to say nothing of the moral objections. For one thing, it would siphon off the country's permanent labor force to a ruinous degree. . . . The second difficulty is the cost, which would run into billions of dollars. Verwoerd appears willing to face up to this, but his voters may not when they grasp the implications of his policy. . . . [In January 1962 Verwoerd announced the establishment of self-rule for a Bantu territory. See "The First Bantu State—the Official Government View," in Section II, below.—Ed.]

In the Afrikaner's case, fear [of the Africans] is accompanied by a terrible inferiority complex and a hatred of everything English. This Anglophobia tragically constricts his outlook. Because the English have done liberal things elsewhere in Africa, he figures liberal solutions are wrong. And what England's Harold Macmillan calls "the wind of change" in Africa speeded the crisis. Ghana is independent; Nigeria soon will be and others will be coming along. [Nigeria became independent in October 1960. Since 1945, when there were only 4 independent nations on the African continent, 25 countries have achieved independence, and 4 more are expected to in 1962-63.—Ed.] The South African Bantus have heard about this, even though probably not one in ten has more than a foggy notion where Ghana is.

Nobody in the Union wants to leap into a desegregated society on five minutes' notice; this would simply not be possible. Moreover, the state of the Bantus is such that although they can organize a Gandhi-like passive resistance, it is difficult to keep it organized. The Bantus can strike and starve Johannesburg anytime. But, having so few resources, they would also starve themselves. However there are new strains within the Nationalist party itself. Many Nationalists are worried about the excesses of apartheid, and a new political alignment may be in the making.

One thing would help immensely: open the doors of the Union to unrestricted white immigration from Europe. Since the Afrikaners defend apartheid on the ground that they fear being "swamped" or "swallowed up," the obvious answer, by their own standards, is to get more white people living in South Africa. Yet this is resisted by the government. New citizens from Sicily, for instance, might not be dependable Nationalist voters.

AN UNEASY REPUBLIC IS BORN [3]

The Republic of South Africa came into being on May 31, 1961, the anniversary of the Treaty of Vereeniging that ended the Boer War in 1902. . . . [It was at this time that the former Union of South Africa was established.] . . . This . . . climax should not blind one to the dangers that face the new republic with its 16 million inhabitants. The great weakness of the Republic is that it was brought about by the votes of little more than half the white population and that the nonwhite majority had no voice in it at all. . . .

The weeks that preceded [the vote for the new Republic] were peaceful . . . But . . . nonwhites had planned a stay-at-home strike for May 29, 30 and 31, together with peaceful demonstrations, their leaders emphasizing their repugnance to any form of violence. . . . [Fearing a repetition of earlier disturbances and] repercussions abroad, the government took drastic measures.

All police leave was stopped. A number of Army units were on partial mobilization. Public meetings without permit were prohibited. The criminal law was hastily amended to empower attorneys general to refuse bail for a period of twelve days at a time, thus removing from the courts their discretion in the matter of bail. Police and army activities were coordinated. For two weeks before May 31 the police systematically raided major African townships and rounded up all idlers who, they said, could be used to intimidate Africans into staying away from work.

[3] From "Uneasy Republic," by Leo Marquard, a South African historian. Baltimore *Sun*. p 12. Je. 20, '61. Reprinted by permission.

The homes of whites who were known to sympathize with nonwhites, Liberal party members and others, were searched in early morning raids for subversive literature, and a few arrests made; and a number of the most active leaders, white and nonwhite, went underground. The police appealed to employers to discharge any employee who stayed at home and threatened ruthless action against anyone encouraging employees to do so or intimidating them if they did not.

These measures induced a state of near panic in the white as well as in the nonwhite population. White women formed pistol clubs and there was an unprecedented run on fire arms and ammunition. Many families laid in stocks of tinned foods in case African messengers should be on strike and unable to deliver food from the stores. The press had details of depots to which people could go for bread and milk, and the police published special telephone numbers that could be dialed in case of emergency.

Despite police activities a large number of African, Coloured (those of mixed race) and Malay workers did in fact stay at home, the pattern varying from town to town. In Johannesburg about 40 per cent of African labor was absent, while in Cape Town it was chiefly Coloured and Malay workers who stayed away.

Nonwhite Attitudes

Generally speaking, the demonstration was about 40 per cent successful; and what there was of it was peaceful. But it was an enforced peace without any guarantee of permanence. Nonwhite attitudes, though still divided, have hardened perceptibly, and the comparative failure of the demonstration has done much to convince younger nonwhites that more drastic methods will have to be used to break the Nationalist party stranglehold. . . .

Afrikaner nationalism has triumphed, but it is a political triumph of, at most, half of the 3 million whites in a population of 16 million. Many whites outside the Nationalist party are prepared to accept a republic outside the Commonwealth, and to make a go of it. But they, like a number of Nationalists, know that race problems cannot be solved on the basis of . . . [a] policy of apartheid.

They know that until South Africa can come to reasonable terms on the race question she will be an outcast among nations, her economic reserves will continue to be threatened, she will have to increase measures for internal security and she will continue to face the prospect of "interference" from outside.

Dr. Verwoerd [the prime minister] has made it clear that he does not intend to budge an inch from his policy, and already the Republic of South Africa has no friend at [the] United Nations except Portugal. Her economic reserves continue to fall and have necessitated import controls. Internal security has become more stringent. The danger of interference from outside—possibly through Angola where Portuguese authority is rapidly waning—becomes daily more real.

An undetermined number of Nationalists are aware of the dangers and would like to replace Dr. Verwoerd by a more moderate leader who would soften the rough edges of apartheid. His position is, however, extremely strong. The constitution of the Nationalist party is federal, and the leader of the party is chosen not by a national conference but by the caucus, that is by the Nationalist members of parliament, most of whom come from the Transvaal and the Free State, solidly behind Dr. Verwoerd. . . .

Moreover, the mystique of Afrikaner nationalism is powerful, combining elements of religion, language, and politics. Even moderate Nationalists would hesitate to take a step that would brand them as enemies of Afrikanderdom. Outside the ranks of the party, businessmen, industrialists and intellectuals are anxiously scanning the horizon for some national, uncommitted leader who might bring about a new political alignment. But all attempts so far have proved fruitless and there is not much hope of immediate success. What is needed, clearly, is someone who can attract those not inconsiderable forces in the country that have come to see the need for consultation with nonwhites.

Afrikaner Control

There is another aspect of Afrikaner nationalism that gives an air of unreality and impermanence to the present situation in South Africa. The extreme wing that now dominates the Nationalist party and South Africa has a natural urge to retain power. It must, therefore, look for new worlds to conquer; and it must be able to conjure up dangers that threaten, if possible, the whole white population, but at least Afrikaner nationalism.

Nationalist leaders have long complained that Afrikaners have an insufficient share of the capital wealth of the country— only 10 per cent, say some, though no one is quite sure how Afrikaner investment is calculated. Political power without financial control may be one of the glittering new worlds that Afrikaner nationalism hopes to dangle before its followers. The market is controlled, say the Nationalists, by "un-South African" people, and these and the English-language press are blamed for an inert market, the withdrawal of capital, the failure to attract capital, and the consequent fall in reserves.

Dangers there are in plenty. There is the ever-present "danger" of being swamped by nonwhites and it does not require much to convince most white South Africans that their safety lies in trusting the "strong man who knows where he is going."

There is the danger that interference from [the] United Nations may try to force white South Africa to adopt an un-South African way of life—which means giving equality to nonwhites. And there is the actual physical danger of invasion from nonwhite states.

While, therefore, there are unmistakable signs that a majority of the population of the Republic longs for a regime in which race tensions will be relaxed, it is clear that the present government will retain power, and this may mean taking greater financial control and imposing more restrictions on individual liberty.

FROM VELD TO CITY [4]

Cutting through the middle of the lives of the black people of South Africa is one of the swiftest and sharpest breaks in the history of any race. It is the crossing from the placid, Stone-Age existence of the tribal reserves to the bustling, twentieth-century cities of modern South Africa—Johannesburg, Durban or Cape Town. It is a contrast that lies inside the minds, to a

[4] From "From Veld to City: The Bantu Drama," by Anthony Sampson, a correspondent for the London *Observer* who once edited a paper for Africans in Johannesburg. New York *Times Magazine*. p 28+. My. 22, '60. Reprinted by permission.

greater or lesser extent, of all black South Africans. This contrast is at the very core of the current South African crisis, for as firmly as the government of Dr. Verwoerd believes that the native people should remain in their primitive tribal state, so do the natives themselves desire passionately and unchangeably to become part of the modern cities.

To white observers, indeed, the metamorphosis of the Africans from country to town is the most fascinating aspect of South Africa. The image of the blanketed tribesman, with bare feet, tribal scars and plugs in his ears, arriving bewildered and innocent in the middle of industrial Johannesburg is one which runs through the white literature of South Africa with a repetition that irritates the Africans themselves. . . .

The theme is, undoubtedly, an evocative one, but it is perhaps less simple than it appears. Educated Africans, who resent the white men's dramatizations of their tribal antecedents, suspect that the writers' interest is based on the old myth of Rousseau's "noble savage"—the quest for some imaginary innocence which sophisticated man has lost. They argue that their own transition has been no more abrupt than that of the English of Shakespeare's time—the "country gulls" who swagger into Elizabethan plays. Above all, they suspect that nearly all white men prefer their Africans to be primitive and untouched, and like to think that black men cannot be assimilated into white cities. In fact, the African intellectuals say most white men believe in apartheid in their hearts.

Certainly, few white visitors could fail to be attracted by the outward appearance of life in the tribal reserves. Only a hundred miles from the industrial cities of Port Elizabeth or Durban, you can see the clusters of plain mud huts, with nothing but grass mats for furniture, and old women pounding maize with tree stumps outside. A Xhosa girl, her hair wound into a headdress of red clay, and her brown arms jangling with rings, walks by the side of the main road, balancing a pitcher on her head, staying erect and unworried as the Chevrolets and Jaguars swish past her.

To the nerve-racked white businessmen living their complex urban lives, it is hardly surprising that the tribal Africans stand for all the peace they miss in their own existence.

Their tribal life appears magnificently unchanged. The community is dominated by two ancient leaders: the chief and the witch doctor. The chief, it is true, has not the gaudy splendor of the West Africans, with their umbrellas, embroidered gowns and rich jeweled headdresses. A South African chief is likely to wear white man's mufti, or a vague, cast-off uniform, with only a ceremonial blanket, a leopard skin or a shield to signify his status. But the chiefs retain a splendid dignity and apparent authority: they rule through a gathering of elders, and when important issues arise they hold a special meeting of the tribe, or *kgotla*, which constitutes a kind of *ad hoc* democratic process. On festive occasions, they hold a beer-drink, sitting around the floor of a mud hut, and passing a calabash of home-brewed beer from man to man.

There are many aspects of this tribal life that are endearing. There is the responsibility of it—the sense of duty to the family, the chief and the tribe. There is the courtesy, the consideration and the dignity of individuals, particularly old men and women. There is the laughter, the peasant wisdom, and the straightforward human values. Even the witch doctor, hung with bones, hides and bangles, is far from a figure of fun. He is, as a missionary doctor will tell you, a home-grown psychoanalyst who can, in a society riddled with fears and superstitions, cure a psychosomatic illness when Western medicine has failed.

But in this attractive-looking community, there is one indication of a fatal flaw: there are no young men, and even among the older generation there is a vast disparity between men and women. The reason is obvious: the dry, cracked land cannot support the men. They go, as soon as they reach manhood, to earn their livings in the gold mines of Johannesburg or the kitchens of Durban, and to send back money to their families.

The lack of men has corrupted the character of tribal life. The pivot of the community is no longer the chief's court, but the little hut, which exists in every small community, called Wenela—from WNLA, the initials of the Witwatersrand Native Labor Association, the organization of mine owners which brings 400,000 Africans every year to the gold mines.

They are taken in train loads for six- or nine-month contracts, and come back with new suits, hats and phonographs. They leave for second contracts, and then, perhaps, they take permanent city jobs, and never come back again.

They leave behind them a community demoralized by their absence. The land, eroded and poor as it is, is not properly cared for. The women, without their husbands, become undisciplined, promiscuous or prey to mysterious mental diseases and imagined pregnancies. Families are disorganized, and the children are often brought up by an aged grandfather or a drunken uncle. Above all, the country remains desperately poor. The 13 per cent of South African land on which the 3 million tribal Africans live was never enough to sustain them; but the system of migratory African labor, while it provides the reserves with pocket money from remittances, insures that the country areas can never be developed properly.

Doctors, however, more than economists, are the ones who can perceive the true misery of the tribal reserves. To the mission doctors who deal with underfed children, fear-ridden mothers and miners sent back with TB, there is nothing romantic about tribal life; it is nasty, brutish and short.

The main cause of African migration is necessity. Ever since Cecil Rhodes devised a poll tax for rural Africans, to insure a labor supply for his diamond mines in Kimberley in the 1870's, Africans have been forced by taxes and poverty to go to work in the cities.

But even without compulsion, many of them would go; it is more than poverty that brings Africans to Johannesburg from as far away as Nyasaland or Mozambique. All the lure and the glory of Johannesburg—*Geoli*, the Golden City—is summed up for Africans in two letters—TJ, standing for "Transvaal Johannesburg"—on the number plates of Johannesburg cars. As the big cars screech past the dry mud huts, the little pot-bellied Zulu or Xhosa children dance up and down with delight, and shout, "Tee Jay! Tee Jay!"

TJ stands for everything that is exciting: not only cars, but skyscrapers, trains, elevators, cinemas and radios. TJ stands for everything that the young tribal recruit sees as he gazes out at the street from the Johannesburg station. But TJ does not mean only the half million whites of Johannesburg and the white men's wonders: indeed, it is noticeable that the raw Africans are never quite as astonished by the "houses on wheels" or the "huts on top of each other" as the white men expect them to be. No, TJ means more than anything else the black metropolis—the city with 700,000 Africans, the biggest black city in the continent.

It is a very different place from white Johannesburg, and to the Europeans it seems far less attractive than the reserves. The "locations," or "townships," where the Africans live are mostly clusters of boxlike brick houses, beginning ten miles southwest of the city center in the area known as the Orlando Complex, and spreading over the brown hillsides in bleak, unvarying rows, like huge chicken farms.

The locations, although they have become more hygienic and less slummy in the past few years, are uniformly dismal. The houses are all single-story, built at minimum cost. Although there is a large power station near by, the rooms in the African townships have no electric light. The roads are unpaved, full of ditches and boulders. The largest building in most locations is the police station, with the administrative offices of the location superintendent next door.

The skyline of bungalows is unbroken, except for billboards advertising beauty cream, corn flakes, or flashlights ("Be safe at night—carry a torch!"). One house is distinguished from another only by its number: a typical African address is 3586B, Orlando West Extension, Johannesburg. The country Africans call a boy born in the city "the son of a number."

But to the Africans who live in Orlando—so named, before the war, after a paternalistic city councilor who laid out the "model township"—there is nothing impersonal about their city. In spite of the police raids, the mass removals and the pass laws designed to circumscribe and control their daily lives, they love the city, and out of it they have built a new and vibrant society.

The streets which seem so impersonal and bleak to the white visitor have, to the Africans, all the nuances and variations of Manhattan or Mayfair. The extensions and postal districts, or the townships named by the municipality after tribal heroes, are quickly renamed by the Africans after snob white districts or American Negro heroes, like "Killarney," or "Satchmo." Many of the bleak numbers turn out to be "shebeens," or illicit African drinking places, with names like "Falling Leaves," "Back o' the Moon" or "Thirty-Nine Steps."

The shebeen might be taken as the cornerstone of this new metropolis, for it is here that the new society is most vocal and expressive. The contrast with the chief's beer-drink in the reserves is a bizarre one. Instead of the chief and elders, sitting on the mud floor, passing a calabash around, the superior shebeens have a mixture of teachers, bus drivers, nurses and gangsters, sitting around a polished mahogany table, drinking European brandy under a kerosene lamp.

There is little connection with the old society: a teacher might turn out to be a chief's nephew, but descendants of the old Zulu royal family are quite likely to end up as messenger boys or domestic servants. The conversation in a sheebeen will not be about tribal customs or chiefly intrigue, but about Hollywood films, football, jazz or Shakespeare. If some newly arrived innocent, perhaps, raised the subject of tribal ritual, he might well be met with a shout of, "Jeez, man, go back to the kraal! We don't want blanket-boys here."

There are, of course, many tribal relics embedded in this new society, particularly among the newly arrived groups. Some, like the Basutos or the Vendas, still in their multicolored blankets, stride through the crowds as if they were among their native mountains.

Tribal myths and superstitions still play their part in urban life. Five years ago a story suddenly became current that a *tokoloshe*—a kind of Zulu imp—had been discovered in Johannesburg, and for two weeks copies of the local African newspaper, *The Bantu World,* were sold out with stories of the *tokoloshe*—which turned out to be an otter.

Sometimes the tribal relics are of a grimmer kind, as when a homemade liquor brew is discovered with bits of flesh mixed in it, supposed to strengthen the courage of its drinkers. Witch doctors still do business in Johannesburg, in musty little shops hung with skins, bones and medicines; and when a paramount chief such as King Cyprian of the Zulus or King Sobhuza of the Swazis comes up to Johannesburg, he is besieged by humble tribesmen and guarded in his small location house by bus drivers or municipal clerks.

These tribal memories are often said by whites to be a sign that Africans will never be assimilated into city life, and the government of Dr. Verwoerd has done everything possible to encourage the continuance of tribal feeling, with special "ethnic grouping" in the layout of the townships, and special entries in the passbooks for each person's chief and tribe.

But to hundreds of thousands of urban Africans these sub-divisions mean nothing: some of them have lived for three generations in the towns, have intermarried among tribes, and speak English and Afrikaans at home. For them, it would be as unthinkable to return to the reserves as for the Afrikaners to return to Holland.

The black cities of South Africa are kept separate from the white cities by all the elaborate devices of apartheid. By day the Africans work in the same offices, factories or shops as the white men, and jostle in the same streets; but every night they are separated, and travel in their segregated trains to their segregated townships.

To the whites, the lives of their black office boys or chauffeurs seem unimaginably separate and isolated from their own. Although African jazz has lately become fashionable among white liberals, very few white South Africans have ever made their way into a shebeen, and even to be found drinking with an African constitutes an offense. But to the urban Africans, the "Europeans" are the ones who seem isolated, in their remote and hidden mansions in the superior suburbs. The Africans no longer feel themselves reliant on white patrons or promoters for their education and cultural development; they see themselves as the heirs of Western civilization, and the "Europeans" as the impostors.

In much of the black metropolis, there is a fearful rootlessness —the other side of the imbalance which shows itself in the reserves. There are too few girls, no land, no freehold rights, broken families; often husbands who work as domestic servants are not allowed, because of the Group Areas Act, to sleep with their wives. And all the time, the townships are subject to the perpetual insecurity which comes from the police state—the threat of being waked at midnight for not having a pass, of being exiled to the farms, of being jailed indefinitely for suspected political views.

All these factors have produced ugly elements in the African townships—violence, gangsters, promiscuity and wild drunkenness. They show themselves at their worst each Christmastime when, maddened with liquor and frustration, the wilder Zulus and Basutos engage in atavistic faction fights, and a score or so are murdered.

But against these grimmer sides, there is much that is infinitely exciting and hopeful about this African "Harlem." "The truest optimism in South Africa," wrote the greatest of South Africa's historians, Dr. [Cornelis Willem] De Kiewiet, "is in the crowded, disease-ridden and crime-infested urban locations." Anyone who spends some time in the shebeens or social gatherings of Orlando, Meadowlands or Sophiatown can understand what he means. The Africans have not, as a race, been demoralized by the white men's cities; they have taken to them with all the enthusiasm of a London Cockney, and in them have built their own society, hierarchies and prides.

Hundreds of thousands of the new Africans are no longer men of two worlds, but of one—the world of the city, *their* city. Out of their varied backgrounds—motorcars, blankets, cinemas, witch doctors, physicians, chiefs, lawyers—they have forged something new, confident and civilized.

Signs of this new amalgam take many forms: the new African jazz blending old monotonous tribal chants with sharp new rhythms from America; the all-African musical *King Kong,* which appeared . . . [in 1959] in Johannesburg . . . [and later in London—Ed.]; the young African writers and journalists who have produced a jazzy, expressive English of their own; even the curious Johannesburg wedding ceremonies, with their mixture of tribal courtesy, Western formality and all-African prolixity.

But the new character can be seen most simply in the urban Africans themselves. Though the whites may view them as clowns, dandies, imitative monkeys, the Africans are fundamentally confident—of themselves, and of their right to Western civilization. The more one sees of them, the more one feels that Dr. Verwoerd, who is determined that they shall have no place in the white men's cities, has bitten off more than he can chew.

SOUTH AFRICA IN PERSPECTIVE [5]

In these past fifty years, South Africa has grown from a country of less than 6 million people to one with a population of about 15 million. Today it is the most industrialized nation on the African continent, with a yearly national income of some $4.5 billion. Its exports top $1.2 billion a year, without counting the gold from South African mines, which nets an additional $600 million or so annually. Rich in diamonds, gold, and uranium mined with the technical skill of the white man and the labor of the African, South Africa since World War II has made particularly striking progress. . . .

In the past decade or so, South African production has increased impressively in most spheres. Great new gold fields have been discovered in the Orange Free State, and modern new towns have sprung up almost overnight to serve them. A uranium industry has come into being and will ultimately net South Africa about $140 million annually from overseas sales. All this urban development has brought thousands of whites and non-whites crowding into the cities from the land, each group anxious to boost its living standards. This new contact and competition between the races, as well as the strain on social and other services such as housing, education, and so forth, particularly for the lesser-paid nonwhites, have considerably complicated an already complex color problem in this country. This problem was not, of course, created by the present Afrikaner Nationalist government, which came to power in 1948. For the problem had been snowballing over the years in a country where nonwhites outnumber whites by four to one. Inherited by this government, the problem nevertheless has come to a climax during its period of office through a variety of circumstances.

Whatever the problems, and whatever the reservoir of African frustration which remains, the government has contributed extensively toward the improvement of African conditions. In the field of African housing, for example, the government points out that in the decade since 1948, it has established 60 new housing areas for Africans, extended 60 existing ones, and planned for expansion in a further 77 areas. During this period, loan

[5] From "South Africa—After 50 years," by John Hughes, staff correspondent. The *Christian Science Monitor*. p 9. Ag. 20, '59. Reprinted by permission.

funds provided by the government have made possible the building of 81,000 houses for urban Africans at a cost of more than $56 million. Additionally a services levy of 35 cents a worker a week has been imposed on employers since 1952 to provide essential services such as roads, water, and lighting within African townships. To date, the government states, it has spent more than $22 million on such items. Additionally, it reports that it spent $140 million up to the end of 1956 on extended and improved railway services to speed African workers to and from their work in the cities.

In terms of education government figures indicate that at the present rate of enrollment in African schools illiteracy will be wiped out in twenty to twenty-five years. It states that the present African literacy rate is 30 per cent, "far higher than in any other African territory." Expenditure on African education, says the government, rose from $2.8 million in 1940 to $14 million in 1950, and then doubled the latter figure to become nearly $28 million by 1958-59. The government's contribution to this is fixed at $18.2 million annually, and the remainder comes from taxes paid by Africans themselves. The total number of pupils enrolled in African schools under government control is about 1.25 million, and there are some 83,000 African children at Roman Catholic schools and 25,000 at other private schools. About 52 per cent of the total number of African children currently are attending schools, says the government.

In addition to this over-all development, the government has various plans for agricultural progress in the African reserves—tribal areas comprising some 13 per cent of the country, which Africans now are being encouraged to look to as a national home. The government reports that it has four hundred white and five hundred African officials training African peasants in farming methods, but that Africans are slow in changing their primitive farming ways. The government has established nine animal breeding centers to improve African livestock, and its engineers have built, or assisted with, 1,200 dams, 2,000 boreholes, 10,000 miles of fencing, and 10,000 miles of road within these African areas. "Nevertheless," says South Africa's official yearbook, "it is obvious that peasant farming alone will no longer support the whole Bantu (African) population." Recently the government set up a $1.4 million investment corporation to stimulate economic development in the African reserves. Although this is only a beginning—and a report by the independent Institute of Race Relations says that the only industries established in the areas in recent years are "a very small sawmill and a very small factory to produce windows, doors, and simple furniture, employing three whites and twelve Africans"—the $1.4 million is a start toward the mammoth task of developing the African areas.

Whites Aid Nonwhites

Meanwhile, among the flow of stories from South Africa today underlining the complexity of the color problem and the unhappy lot of many nonwhites, there are other, less-publicized stories of white and nonwhite cooperation and of kindnesses shown nonwhites by whites, and vice versa. There are instances, for example, of great courage and devotion on the part of African servants to their white employers in times of disturbance or danger. One white family credits its safety during recent floods in Natal largely to the steadfastness of an African maid. Africans frequently have rescued from various dangers white children placed in their care. Similarly, many white South Africans rally instantly when disaster overtakes Africans, flooding emergency centers with clothes, food, and money. One African who lost his legs while trying to save an elderly man in front of a train received a total of $2,800 in various-sized donations from people all over the country. . . . The government-supporting Dutch Reformed Church budgets more than $1.8 million annually for mission work among nonwhites in southern Africa and has 250,000 communicants among its "daughter," or nonwhite churches. The Dutch Reformed Church has organized a Christian Literature Fund aiming at more than $8 million expenditure to spread Christian literature among nonwhites. It operates hospitals, schools, and industrial institutions with its mission work. . . .

Meanwhile, the government states that it . . . is doing its utmost to encourage the training of Africans for service within their own communities. . . . All told, the government estimates that it, together with provincial and municipal administrations, is spending more than $112 million a year on the welfare of the African population. Thus, though problems loom and South

Africa's races are far from united fifty years after their nation's beginning, these are some of the facts over which the country can rejoice when it takes time out . . . [in 1960] to celebrate its Golden Jubilee.

THE FABULOUS ECONOMY [6]

"So little done, so much to do," lamented Cecil John Rhodes as he lay dying. Though he had planted Britain's flag firmly across southern Africa, won fame and fortune in both business and politics, and ensured a measure of immortality through his legacy for future scholars, his great dream of a vast economic empire spreading without limit from its base in the fabulous African diamond mines eluded him. But today, from the grandeur and loneliness of a tomb, hewn from the rock in the Matopos, high above the Southern Rhodesian plateau, the spirit of Rhodes might flutter out in all directions and see how the empire came into being.

It took another ambitious dreamer, Sir Ernest Oppenheimer, and since his death in 1957, his son, Harry Frederick Oppenheimer, to achieve the reality. The reality consists of the biggest and most profitable conglomeration of gold mines, diamond mines, and copper mines, plus many other industrial ventures, ever put together. The Oppenheimer empire, which may be called the "Anglo American Group" has two major bases—the Anglo American Corporation of South Africa, Ltd., and De Beers Consolidated Mines, Ltd., which, in turn, have fingers in some 150 other companies. . . . The combined net assets of all the companies run to $2,423,070,000, and profits before taxes last year [1959] ran to $359,382,000, profits after taxes to $271,074,000.

This empire sprawls across Africa from Cape Town to the shores of Lake Victoria, reaches into Europe and the United States, and even has influence in the Soviet Union. Last year the gold mines directly controlled by Anglo American Corporation (it also has investments in the mines of other South African producers) turned out 30 per cent of the Union of South Africa's 18.75 million fine ounces of gold (which, in turn, was 58.5 per cent of the free world's production). Anglo American also produced

⁶ Reprint of "Harry Oppenheimer's Industrial Africa," by the editors of *Fortune*. *Fortune*. 61:152-65. My. '60. Reprinted from the May 1960 issue of *Fortune* Magazine by special permission; © 1960 Time Inc.

22 per cent of the Union's 6,440 tons of uranium and 40 per cent of the 40 million tons of coal. Its copper mines in the Federation of Rhodesia and Nyasaland will extract 58 per cent of Rhodesia's 570,000 tons of copper this year. From the De Beers mines came about 4 million carats of diamonds, accounting for $95.2 million of the record $252 million in natural diamond sales in 1959. And, through its subsidiary, the Diamond Corporation, and through five other sales subsidiaries, De Beers controlled the distribution of almost all the remaining $156.8 million worth of natural diamonds.

This is only the beginning. The companies in the group also mine cobalt, iron pyrites, lead, zinc, asbestos, monozite, manganese, titanium, Vanadium, and other minerals. They process much of what they take from the ground in their own refineries and sell the finished products through their own selling companies. They have operating and investment interests in the production of explosives, iron and steel, electricity, refractory products, roofing, diamond tools, limestone, cotton yarn, tire cord, cement, metal alloys, food, clay pipe and fittings, and wood and forest products among others. They have huge investment portfolios. They run financial and banking houses, do management and engineering work, conduct extensive research programs in a variety of fields, maintain large and active prospecting organizations, and have enormous real estate holdings.

Not the least of these other ventures is the construction and maintenance of whole cities. Since gold, diamonds, and other rare minerals are most often found in desolate wastes far from civilization, Anglo American must bring civilization to its mines. In this way, it may well be fostering one of the most important revolutions in Africa, for it is providing the jobs and the wealth that will build Africa's future. Just a few months ago the *Times* of London told South Africa's Nationalist prime minister, Dr. Hendrik Verwoerd, that Anglo American's chief, Harry Oppenheimer, was just as important to the country as he. Concluded the *Times:* "Dr. Verwoerd governs a country which without the mines would rank nowhere in the hierarchy of nations. Mr. Oppenheimer manages the assets which give South Africa its international position."

A Giant on His Own

At fifty-one, small, dark Harry Oppenheimer is the man who runs this vast operation. He is a man of enormous wealth, owning some 56,540 shares of Anglo American Corporation, and an unspecified but large block in De Beers. In addition, he is chairman of both key companies plus a host of smaller ones. He was thoroughly trained to take charge: while still in his teens, he became a familiar figure with his father around Anglo American's headquarters in Johannesburg, and was tutored at Oxford's Christ Church College by Britain's famed economist, Sir Roy Harrod. During the war, while Harry Oppenheimer was an intelligence officer with a far-ranging South African armored-car regiment in the Western Desert, Sir Ernest's letters to him were filled with corporation affairs.

Like Rhodes and Sir Ernest, Harry Oppenheimer had an active and even brilliant political career. From 1948 until 1957, when Sir Ernest's death forced him to devote full time to business, he represented the Kimberley constituency in the South African parliament (a seat held also by Sir Ernest). A "frontbencher," he was the United (Opposition) party's spokesman on financial affairs, and his answer to the government's budget message became an annual event in Cape Town that filled the galleries to overflowing. Though he has now withdrawn from active participation in politics, he still maintains a vital interest in government. And his growing disgust with the United party's parroting of the Nationalists' apartheid program has caused him to join the new Progressive party, which seeks some enlightened solutions to South Africa's distressing racial problems.

"For Heaven's Sake, Make Decisions"

In business, too, Harry Oppenheimer is proving that he has ideas of his own. His father concentrated all power in his own hands and considered Anglo American his own domain. Sir Ernest even assumed that anyone who happened to be around his offices naturally worked for him. He once went up to a man he had spotted and asked if the fellow was happy working for Anglo American or if there was something Sir Ernest could do to make life pleasanter for him. The man turned out to be the United States Ambassador to South Africa.

Harry has put administration on a businesslike basis. While the group may still have the feel of a family company, there are now channels through which everything flows swiftly and efficiently. And there are people to see that things get done without having to check back with the chairman. Said Harry to a subordinate recently, "For heaven's sake, make decisions. I'd rather you made a mistake than no decision at all." As an old-time Anglo American executive reflected recently, "The essential difference is this: Sir Ernest was a genius. He made spot decisions, based chiefly on experience but sometimes containing the elements of intuition and hunch. Sometimes he was not really sure why he made a specific decision. Now Harry, with his splendid mind and his fine education, is different. He has his father's flair for finance and his intuitive gift. But Harry suppresses the hunch in favor of logical examination of a problem. Harry knows precisely why he makes every decision."

By delegating authority, Harry Oppenheimer has freed his hand for making major expansionist moves. He arranged, for instance, the purchase by De Beers of a 50 per cent interest in big Williamson Diamonds Ltd., of Tanganyika (something Sir Ernest strove vainly to do) and loaned the Tanganyika government part of the money to buy the other half-interest. And, this past January, he negotiated an agreement with the Russians, who had made major diamond finds in Siberia, for De Beers's Diamond Corporation to market Soviet diamonds in the West.

Diamonds!

This world-wide stabilization of the diamond market would have warmed the heart of Cecil Rhodes, who came to South Africa in 1871 at the height of the great diamond rush. Diamonds were first found in the mid-sixties along the Orange and Vaal rivers. Then the glittering gems were discovered in huge quantities on a sixty-square-mile tract made up of three farms: Bultfontein, Dorstfontein, and Vooruitzicht (now the city of Kimberley). The owners of Vooruitzicht were two Boer brothers, Johannes Nicolaas and Diederick Arnoldus de Beer. They made no fortune from diamonds, though they left their name to the greatest of the diamond companies, and their farm was the site of the two greatest discoveries: the De Beers and the Kimberley mines.

In 1873, Rhodes bought a small claim at the De Beers mine, and in 1880 formed the De Beers Mining Company, which soon acquired the whole mine. He then cast his eye on nearby Kimberley, which was controlled by another young Englishman, Barney Barnato. Rhodes first bought a claim that cut across Barnato's Kimberley Central holdings, traded it to Barnato for a share in Kimberley Central, and then bought Kimberley Central shares until he owned enough to force Barnato to come to terms. In 1888, Barnato turned his stock over to Rhodes in exchange for a large block of a new company, De Beers Consolidated Mines, Ltd., organized by Rhodes, and a seat on its board as a permanent governor. When a group of Kimberley stockholders challenged the merger, Rhodes simply liquidated Kimberley Central, purchasing its assets for £5,338,650 (the canceled check, framed, still hangs on the wall of De Beers headquarters in Kimberley).

Once he had the two mines, Rhodes's next step was to capture the distribution of diamonds and stabilize the world's demand. He felt that the number of diamonds sold each year should just about equal the number of engagements; this would keep the price high and the supply tight. By the mid-1890's he had won over other diamond producers, and had set up the Diamond Syndicate. Meanwhile, he used his fortune from diamonds to exploit a new opportunity. After gold was discovered in the Transvaal in 1886, Rhodes bought heavily into the mining claims on the Rand. He also turned north, and began to carry his dreams of empire into the wilds of Rhodesia, the present source of copper and coal. Then it was that his time ran out; he died in 1902 at the age of forty-eight, with the makings of an empire in his hands, but its consolidation far from complete.

As Rhodes's body was being borne on its long journey north to its tomb in the Matopos, another young man arrived at the diamond mines in Kimberley. He was twenty-one-year-old German-born Ernest Oppenheimer, who, after a five-year apprenticeship in London, had been sent out to Africa to represent

Anton Dunkelsbuhler & Company, a leading member of the Diamond Syndicate. Within a year after his arrival, a new diamond mine was discovered three hundred miles away, near Pretoria. The De Beers company, though still in control of the diamond business, was at first not interested. But Ernest Oppenheimer went to take a look, and persuaded Dunkelsbuhler to invest heavily in the new mine, the Premier, where the world's largest diamond, the Cullinan—3,106 carats uncut—was later found. By the time De Beers realized its mistake, it had to buy out Dunkelsbuhler to gain control of the mine, and young Oppenheimer received a share of his company's profit on the deal.

The De Beers outfit did not forget this incident, and for years Oppenheimer was *persona non grata* with its management and owners. So he turned from diamonds to gold. Most gold mining was then under way on the Central Rand; an American mining engineer, William Lincoln Honnold, however, was sure that there were rich deposits on the East Rand, and he won Oppenheimer to this idea. Together, they persuaded some American and British financiers, including J. P. Morgan & Company, to put up £500,000, or half the necessary capital. Oppenheimer himself and some South African friends put up the remaining £500,000, and the venture was incorporated in 1917 as Anglo American Corporation of South Africa, Ltd. The veins of gold on the East Rand proved to be fabulous. Then, turning to the West Rand, the syndicate found even richer gold deposits.

With the wealth of gold to back him, Oppenheimer could now deal with De Beers. Some years earlier he had explored the alluvial beaches of German South-West Africa, having heard reports of fabulous diamond finds in the sands. Now, with the end of World War I and with South African mandate of the former German territory, he moved to take over these beaches. By 1920 his Consolidated Diamond Mines of South-West Africa was in control of the alluvial fields. He then maneuvered into control of the contract to run the Diamond Syndicate, then began to buy large blocks of De Beers shares on the open market, and press for a seat on its board. De Beers' chairman, P. Ross Frames, held out against Oppenheimer. But, by 1926, Frames had to surrender. He resigned and Oppenheimer, by then Sir Ernest (he was knighted in 1921), was elected to fill the vacant seat. Three years later he was named chairman. Thus was joined the gold of Anglo American Corporation with the diamonds of De Beers.

Immediately Sir Ernest was faced with the consequences of the world-wide depression. The only solution for the diamond men, as far as he could see, was to keep diamonds off the market; and the only way this could be done was for one company to own all the diamonds. So, Sir Ernest reorganized the Diamond Syndicate into a new company, the Diamond Corporation, under the control of De Beers. It would buy all the diamonds of every producer and then dole the gems out as demand dictated. For years the going was rough; demand was at a low ebb; but by the mid-1930's it picked up and it has been high ever since.

Sir Ernest was not content to have only gold and diamonds going at the same time. Like Rhodes, he was continually engaged in a multiplicity of activities that would bewilder a lesser man. In 1924 he picked up another of Rhodes's dreams and moved into Rhodesia, where he found huge copper deposits. From gold to diamonds to copper, Sir Ernest expanded and broadened the activities of Anglo American. He bought up the properties of other producers when he could, developed new properties whenever they appeared, and, as holes appeared in his empire, he filled them by moving into new fields.

The $35 Ceiling

This empire, which Sir Ernest put together around his Anglo American Corporation and Rhodes's De Beers, is the one that Harry Oppenheimer runs today. In diamonds, it has, to all intents, a monopoly. De Beers produces nearly 40 per cent of the world's diamonds at its ten mines, which include the world's richest, the alluvial fields of the Consolidated Diamond Mines of South-West Africa. And, through its Diamond Corporation, it controls the marketing of most of the rest. Through agreements with other diamond producers, it buys up all the output and then seeks to sell the stones, through either its Diamond Trading Company (gems) or Industrial Distributors, Ltd. (industrial diamonds). With this control of the world supply, the Diamond Corporation can not only dictate how many diamonds will be sold in any one year but can also just about set prices. And,

with current demand what it is, buyers don't even get a choice
of stones: they take what De Beers offers.

The importance of the diamonds, however, is actually overshadowed by the biggest of Anglo American's ventures, in gold
and uranium. The fourteen gold mines stretch across the Rand
in the Transvaal to the fabulous Orange Free State gold fields
discovered just before World War II, and include one of the
world's richest, the President Brand, near Welkom in the Free
State. The President Brand, however, will soon be surpassed by
two other Anglo American mines in the Free State, the Free
State Geduld and Western Holdings. These, in turn, will be
topped when production begins in 1962 at the company's Western
Deep Levels in the Transvaal, which will work two ore veins,
at six thousand feet and at ten thousand feet below the earth's
surface. But despite the richness of these veins, Anglo American
is caught in a squeeze; its mining costs have been rising, but the
price of gold is largely fixed at the equivalent of $35 per ounce—
the price paid by the United States Treasury. To offset this
squeeze in gold Anglo American has of recent years made the
most of the fact that some of its gold mines are also rich in
uranium. In cooperation with atomic energy authorities in the
United States, Britain, and South Africa, the group is heavily
involved in extracting and processing uranium for both military
and civilian use.

In copper Anglo American has to contend with an opposite
kind of problem: i.e., copper prices are far from "fixed." The
empire's six copper companies include one of the world's richest—
Nchanga Consolidated—and produce more than half the metal
coming from the Rhodesian Copperbelt. Its refining facilities in
Rhodesia are second only to those of Kennecott Copper at Magna,
Utah. The profits from these operations tend to fluctuate sharply
with the gyrations of copper prices. In 1957, for example, when
prices were high, copper added $44 million to the after-tax profits
of Anglo American-De Beers. A year later, when the price fell,
copper profits totaled a mere $16 million.

Despite this $28-million decline, however, the group's over-all
earnings went down only $10 million. The reason is that Anglo
American reaps the benefits of enormous diversification. It mines
almost 40 per cent of the Union of South Africa's coal at its
eleven Union mines and, from its Wankie Colliery in Southern

Rhodesia, all the coal in the Rhodesian Federation. Its coal mining ties in with its interests in iron and steel and in other manufacturing. And to this should be added the fact that Anglo American is now one of the biggest bankers in South Africa. In 1955, as one answer to the Union's desperate need for a short-term money market, Anglo American set up Union Acceptances Ltd., patterned after some of the great banking houses of London. Since then it has established other merchant banks, in Rhodesia and in Switzerland, and has formed the Discount House of South Africa.

"Where Is the Place of Understanding?"

With this expansion, it is not difficult to see why the Anglo American group makes money, and by the constant reinvestment of funds contributes to Africa's development and growth. For where Harry Oppenheimer goes, there goes civilization. Out of the deserts and the jungles rise whole cities to house and maintain Anglo American's 160,000 workers, of whom 140,000 are Africans. In the Orange Free State the group has built from scratch the city of Welkom, with a population of fifty thousand. In the heart of the alluvial beaches of South-West Africa it has erected the town of Oranjemund for its diamond miners. New towns have also sprouted throughout Northern Rhodesia. And in most cases the companies provide schools, hospitals and medical care, and recreational facilities practically free of charge.

Yet, for all its attempts to improve the lot of its workers, Anglo American remains caught in the middle of Africa's unsolved problem—the problem of white versus black. Wages for African miners have been raised consistently to about $805 a year in the Rhodesian Copperbelt. But the average white miner earns $5,320 a year; and even where the Oppenheimer companies have attempted to improve the job status of African native labor, they have met, in most cases, the stubborn opposition of both white unions and governments. When the Oppenheimers decided to build model family communities for the native workers in the Union of South Africa, for instance, the Nationalist government declared it wanted no new "Black Spots" created: the companies should use migratory native workers only. After much heated debate, Anglo American was finally allowed to provide family housing for 3 per cent of its native labor force.

In addition to the racial issue, or rather because of it, Anglo American faces the continuous threat of rampant nationalism. While it has never yet had its properties expropriated, there is continual agitation in Tanganyika, for example, for the expulsion of Europeans. Such agitation makes no sense logically, for without foreign capital there could be no development. But emotion is more important than logic, and Anglo American inherits all the problems arising from the legacy of a hundred years of white rule and a pressing African drive for independence.

Harry Oppenheimer, more than most industrialists, is aware of these issues and wants to mitigate them.

It seems to me [he says] that, from whatever angle one approaches this complicated problem, one comes back to the conclusion that constitutional changes are essential by which both Europeans and Africans would be guaranteed against the passing of unfair discriminatory legislation based on race. Once it has been admitted that Africans must be allowed and encouraged to develop economically, culturally, and politically to the full extent of their capabilities, no other conclusion is possible.

But Oppenheimer is also aware of the real difficulties of finding solutions. For all his wealth and success, he is fond of quoting from the Book of Job: "Iron is taken out of the earth, and brass is molten out of the stone. . . . The stones of it are the place of sapphires, and it hath dust of gold. . . . But where shall wisdom be found? And where is the place of understanding?"

THE PRESENT ECONOMIC CRISIS [7]

On May 31 [1961] South Africa became an independent republic outside the Commonwealth. From the political standpoint, this event must be regarded as the culmination of the struggle of Afrikaner nationalism to return to the state of affairs that existed in the Transvaal before the Anglo-Boer War. The prime minister promised his supporters that this was the final step needed to bring about a union between English and Afrikaans-speaking South Africans and thus lay the foundations for a rapid solution of the wider race problem. But if any hopes

[7] From "South Africa Faces Its Crisis," by a South African correspondent. *Banker.* 111:405-9. Je. '61. Reprinted by permission.

were raised then, they have since been shown to have been sadly misplaced. . . .

In the early years following . . . [the Nationalists' rise to power] the South African economy was particularly prosperous. The postwar boom continued into the period of the Korean War, while a growing awareness of the great wealth of the new West Rand and Free State gold fields acted as a magnet to overseas investors. The economic prospects were so favorable that at this stage there appeared little need to worry about wider political issues. . . .

It is only lately, indeed, that South Africa's strong economic constitution has been showing signs of serious deterioration, necessitating the emergency measures which are aimed principally at halting the heavy drain on the country's foreign exchange reserves. It is, of course, a country richly endowed with all the ingredients necessary for industrial prosperity—and it was this great economic promise of prosperity that postponed for so long the now rapidly deepening crisis of confidence in the country's future. . . .

It was not surprising, therefore, that the news of South Africa's withdrawal from the Commonwealth was followed not only by a further loss of overseas confidence, but by a widespread deterioration in local confidence stemming from the general uncertainty about the implications of the break. . . . (Legislation has been introduced both in South Africa and in the United Kingdom instituting a twelve months period of grace during which officials of both countries will be able to study the implications of South Africa's break with the Commonwealth and possibly negotiate bilateral agreements. Meanwhile the status quo will be retained.)

The country is faced with a crisis of confidence as great as any in its history. Politically its leaders have chosen isolation. It now remains to be seen whether Dr. Verwoerd has decided in favor of economic isolation as well. He may well have little other choice if he is determined to continue rigidly along his chosen path. . . .

The concept of a siege economy is not without some attractions to a government determined to turn its back on world opinion. For some time now there has been a significant debate on the question whether South Africa could sustain itself without foreign capital. One observer, the chairman of the Industrial Development Corporation, Dr. van Eck, has indeed expressed the view that not only could South Africa do without foreign capital, but might, in fact, be better off without it. The question is not so much whether a siege economy is possible, but rather at what cost it can be achieved. In this regard the significant determinants are: (a) South Africa's ability to generate savings sufficient to provide not only for its own development but also for contractual repayments of certain overseas debt and—so long as the efflux of private capital continues—for repayment of those borrowings as well; (b) South Africa's assured world market for basic exports, gold, diamonds, base metals, wool and the like, and to a less extent, the British market for fruit and wines; (c) the realities of boycotts and prohibitions on manufactured goods, which have in any case closed many markets, especially in Africa, to South African products. . . .

The harm caused by Dr. Verwoerd's official intransigence is now becoming painfully real. While it may be possible for the government to prevent the present tense situation from leading to violence, the mounting number of official provocative acts—police raids, mass arrests, partial mobilization and alarmist statements—are rapidly creating an atmosphere of near-hysteria that could do lasting harm to the country as a whole. The government appears to have lost its nerve and is now taking panic measures. The political situation must therefore remain dangerous and so long as that is so the economy will be under strain; only by coming to terms with reality can South Africa pass into more tranquil times. And in those terms the siege economy becomes as much a part of the dream world of Dr. Verwoerd as his ideal of complete apartheid.

AN INTRODUCTION TO SOUTH AFRICA TODAY [8]

The series of shocks which reverberated through the Union of South Africa early in 1960 suggested that the Union's fiftieth anniversary might be a turning point in its history. After seven months of worrisome headlines about a spreading boycott, South Africans were confronted in rapid succession with British Prime

[8] From "Apartheid in a Hostile World," by Vernon McKay, professor of African studies, School of Advanced International Studies of Johns Hopkins University. *Africa Special Report* (now *Africa Report*). 5:3-4+. D. '60. Reprinted by permission.

Minister Macmillan's "wind of change" speech to parliamentarians in Cape Town on February 3 [explained below]; the fatal Sharpeville riot on March 21, in which seventy-two Africans were killed and at least 186 wounded by police fire; a severe plunge in the value of shares on the Johannesburg stock exchange totaling £501 million between January 1 and March 31; a startling condemnation by the United States State Department less than forty-eight hours after Sharpeville; the seizure and imprisonment without trial of nearly two thousand South Africans under a state of emergency proclaimed on March 30; a denunciation by the United Nations Security Council on April 1; and the attempt to assassinate Prime Minister Hendrik F. Verwoerd on April 9.

In the decade before this succession of catastrophes, most South African whites, under continuous pressure from world opinion, had developed a protective armor which enabled them to ignore the United Nations and other external critics, at least on the surface. This was true not only of Afrikaans-speaking supporters of the Nationalist party, which controls the government, but also of English-speaking members of the opposition United party. The English-language press, which campaigns against the present government, frequently joined the Nationalists in attacking foreign meddling in South African affairs.

The big question after Sharpeville was whether the shocks of 1960 had cracked the walls of apartheid. It did not appear so on May 20 when Dr. Verwoerd . . . declared that the government saw no reason to depart from its policy of separate development of the races. . . . Many enemies of the government . . . feel that external pressures only help the Nationalists win votes by patriotic denunciations of foreign intervention. Both conservatives and liberals, from Johannesburg to Stellenbosch, are inclined to ask whether foreign attacks on apartheid really produce any lasting effect, and, in particular, whether they are strong enough to force a change in government policy. It is not an easy question to answer.

South Africa's whites, who are the primary subject of this article, numbered 3,067,000 in mid-1959. They enjoy one of the highest standards of living in the world, and their prosperity has indirectly benefited the country's 9,751,000 Africans or Bantus, 1,450,000 Coloureds of mixed blood, and 405,000 Asians. More advanced than most Africans north of the Limpopo in material

ways, the Union's nonwhites naturally find racial discrimination
all the more frustrating. . . .

After fifteen years of hostility from the UN General Assembly,
South Africans were partially inured to the first attack on them
from another UN organ, the Security Council. The unexpected
State Department criticism proved quite disturbing; but since it
came within forty-eight hours after Sharpeville, it was generally
regarded as a premature and immature prejudgment of the situation, and as a power politics play in the American popularity
contest with the Russians for Afro-Asian favor. The boycott
movement, after arousing initial alarm, had moved off the front
pages and was termed an empty threat. But British Prime Minister Macmillan's celebrated "wind of change" speech on February 3 was big news for nearly seven weeks. Numerous observers
contended that the impact of the speech was so great that "South
Africa would never be the same again." It therefore provides a
valuable test case of the effect of external pressures on South
Africa.

The text of the speech gives little indication of why it aroused
such a tempest. It is a delicate balance of sympathy and criticism
which begins with praise, turns to warning, and ends on a note
of friendship. South Africans tended to overlook Macmillan's
opening remarks on the economic interdependence between the
Union and the United Kingdom. Instead, they concentrated on
his "wind of change" blowing through the African continent, his
remarks on the "African national consciousness" which we must
all "come to terms with," and his pointed warning that there
were aspects of South African policies which "make it impossible"
for the United Kingdom to support the Union "without being
false to our own deep convictions about the political destinies of
free men."

The immediate reaction to Macmillan was one of calm, but
it was calm before the storm. Prime Minister Verwoerd, in an
impromptu but moderate reply, called for justice for the white
man too. In its leading editorial the next morning, the government organ, *Die Transvaler,* quietly dismissed the subject by
noting that two distinguished statesmen with different backgrounds had spoken and that their views had naturally varied.

Three days later, the storm broke in flamboyant and exaggerated banner headlines in South Africa's most widely read news-

paper, the Johannesburg *Sunday Times* of February 7: "Mac Changes Political Face of Africa—Shattering Impact of Visit Analyzed." Calling Macmillan's address "the gravest international setback the Nationalist government has suffered since it came to power in 1948," the *Sunday Times,* in three leading articles, exploited to the limit one new "fact" it claimed to have discovered, namely that "Mr. Macmillan told Dr. Verwoerd that Britain would no longer be able to vote for South Africa at the United Nations." . . .

Even if there was little new in Macmillan's speech, it was quite startling that a British prime minister, while a guest of a Nationalist government, should speak bluntly on delicate issues. To add insult to injury, the heresy came from a distinguished Conservative rather than a "hopeless" Labour leader. The cabinet members must have been aware of the rapid pace of change in Africa, but they evidently expected their guest to be circumspect in speaking about it while in the Union. As for the Afrikaner rank and file, as well as many English-speaking whites, it is perhaps true that they were so out of touch with African trends that they were really surprised to find the "wind of change" so near. . . .

Coming at the end of seven weeks of controversy over Macmillan's views, the Sharpeville shooting on March 21 and the angry world-wide reaction to it shook South Africa to the core. It seemed to confirm that the wind of change had at last reached the Union. The Sharpeville demonstration against rigorous pass laws was the most disastrous of a number of outbursts organized by the uncompromising Pan-Africanist Congress under the leadership of Robert Mangaliso Sobukwe, a university language instructor who was sentenced to three years in prison after the March rioting. His new radical organization has grown swiftly in the past year at the expense of the more moderate African National Congress.

The world soon learned, however, that white South Africans still had the power and the will to rule. The government's reaction to nation-wide reports of African ferment and to rumors of imminent pressures from overseas was to proclaim a state of emergency on March 30. Swiftly the police rounded up and imprisoned nearly two thousand political suspects, including about one hundred whites, an action shrouded in secrecy because the emergency regulations made it an offense punishable by up to £500 fine and five years' imprisonment to mention the name of anyone detained under the emergency regulations.

Verwoerd Strengthened

The emergency measures broke the back of African resistance for the time being. With the leaders in jail, even passive resistance cannot be organized effectively. It should be noted, moreover, that only a limited amount of white power was used. In addition to a mobile police force, South Africa has a small permanent force of army commando units, air and naval forces, a large citizen force of white citizens who undergo periodic training, and *Skiet Kommandos* of relatively untrained Afrikaner farmers and townsmen who like the citizen force, are subject to call by the Minister of Defense.

The government's position was also strengthened by the attempt to kill the prime minister, for it had the psychological effect of elevating Dr. Verwoerd in Afrikaner esteem at a critical moment when his policy was under heavy fire. Although he was admired by many Afrikaners as a strong leader, he had been considered an intellectual rather than a man of the people. When he "shed his blood" for them, he somehow became one of the people for the first time. As the *Transvaler* expressed it, "Blood Brings Unity." . . .

With the iron hand of the government in firm control, the time came for thoughts of a velvet glove. On April 19, during the incapacity of the prime minister, the minister of lands, forestry and public works, Paul O. Sauer, made a widely publicized speech at Humansdorp. The "old book" of South African history had been closed a month ago at Sharpeville, he said, and South Africa must reconsider her whole approach to the "native question." He qualified this sweeping statement, however, by adding that although there must be an important change in the practical application of government policy, "it will not mean a deviation from the set policy."

When the *Rand Daily Mail* blew the "new deal" up into a party split, the glare of this exaggerated and ill-timed publicity naturally forced the Nationalists to close ranks. Minister of External Affairs Eric Louw told parliament the next day that "Basically the government's policy remains unchanged . . . if any statement is to be made in regard to basic policy that statement will be made by the prime minister." . . .

Many well-educated Nationalists are highly critical of "Verwoerdism." . . . One hears private attacks on the prime minister expressed in strong terms. But when it comes to public action rather than private talk . . . [loyalty to their own] cultural group usually keeps . . . [critics] from bolting the party. . . . A second weakness of new dealers is inherent in their tactical position. Their criticism is not directed at apartheid but only at the government's methods of implementing the policy. . . .

The pro-government propaganda in the Afrikaans press was a third obstacle to the new dealers. In commenting on warnings from the chairmen of several great corporations, the Afrikaans press soft-pedaled their criticism and emphasized their confidence in the country's economy in the long-range future. This was also true of radio reports of the South African Broadcasting Corporation, which began to disseminate partisan Nationalist propaganda after the emergency was declared. *Die Transvaler* reassured its readers on May 30 that even if the value of shares on the Johannesburg stock exchange had declined by £600 million, the only people who lost anything were the very small percentage who panicked and sold.

Congo Dramatized

Another Afrikaans press technique during the emergency was to play up Congo tribal riots, the Mau Mau revival in Kenya, the Rhodesia-Nyasaland troubles, white emigration from the Congo and Kenya to the Union, and support for South Africa from the United States in the form of numerous letters from white racists in the Deep South. The object was evidently to convince Afrikaners that apartheid was their only salvation. (It should be pointed out, however, that many Afrikaners must also have been reading the English press during this period because the main government-supporting Afrikaans newspapers have a circulation of only 352,000, in contrast to 1,626,000 for the English papers.)

Finally, the efforts of the reformers were sidetracked in June by the rise of the republic issue as the main controversy. . . .

For tactical reasons, the opposition parties decided to wage a vigorous fight to reject a republic in the October 5 referendum, partly on the grounds that a vote for a republic was a vote for Verwoerd. After the return of Eric Louw from the Commonwealth Prime Ministers Conference in May, the United and Progressive parties, supported by the English press, also argued that a South African republic would not be readmitted to the Commonwealth and that it therefore would suffer economically through the loss of imperial preferences. The republicans nonetheless won the referendum with a majority of 52 per cent.

Future of Apartheid

Although the future of apartheid is complicated by many imponderables, the basic element at the moment is the apparent *power* and *will* of the whites to continue to rule, at least in the "white" areas. The problem would be simpler if apartheid were only a slogan to win votes. But it is far more than that. It has been built up into an emotional ideology. Its basic assumption is that separate development to enable Africans to rise to the top in their own sphere is not only possible and moral, but, most important of all, is the only way to save the whites from being swamped by a four-to-one nonwhite majority.

The theory of apartheid has a number of basic flaws. It is economically impracticable because, as many South Africans say, "you can't unscramble eggs." It is politically unrealistic because, in an age when self-determination is sweeping Africa, only a miracle could persuade black men to accept permanently a white man's plans for black destiny, no matter what its merits. Moreover, even if apartheid succeeded in moving many Africans into the reserves, the white areas would still have a black majority.

Present Nationalist thought attempts to meet this dilemma by suggesting that Africans remaining in the white areas would be given political rights in the reserves or self-governing "Bantustans." More reflective Nationalists realize that this fanciful idea is only a politician's dream, and a few have already conceded that the blacks in the white areas must ultimately be given full and equal rights. In their view, the South Africa of the future might became a federation of several autonomous black Bantustans and one racially integrated state, in which the ratio of black and white would be less unequal. This scheme has advocates in several circles, including a small group at the Potchefstroom University for Christian Higher Education. . . .

Farsighted supporters of the government concede that the policy may fail. In that case, they say, the government will have to "rethink" the whole situation. They contend, however, that apartheid has thus far been largely a theory, and they want to put it into practice with a program to develop the reserves even further than contemplated in the £110 million proposals recommended by the Tomlinson Commission in 1955. Privately, a few go further and say that the present policy is only a transitional one to get the country over a difficult period until white attitudes change. On rare occasions it is even said that apartheid may in one sense be "preparing the way for integration." The argument behind this heresy is that if apartheid is successful there will be many able African judges, administrators, doctors, businessmen, and others capable of holding their own in white company; in that event, South Africans might realize for the first time that blacks are not so different from whites.

II. APARTHEID AND AFTER

EDITOR'S INTRODUCTION

Apartheid, the official policy of the government of South Africa, is defined and debated in this section. Briefly, as used by the government, the term means racial segregation, or separate development, under which the whites and Africans are encouraged to develop separate societies, even independent states, according to their own traditions. Further refinements of the term and the inconsistencies of the policy it outlines are dealt with below.

Recent background events relating to apartheid are first sketched in an *Atlantic Monthly* report. The meaning of the policy in its many intimate human details, so far as Africans are concerned, is given by an African journalist, Nathaniel Nakasa, in "The Human Meaning of Apartheid." The pass system, the most obvious manifestation of the policy, is explained next by a Johannesburg correspondent for the *Scotsman,* George Clay. Notes on apartheid as it applies to education and trade unions follow.

Harry Oppenheimer, the industrialist and chairman of the mining and diamond combine described in "The Fabulous Economy," in Section I, above, explains why he is against the present government policy in "Why Apartheid Will Not Work." An American reporter takes issue in part with Oppenheimer and pleads for greater American pressure on the South African government.

In the next two articles of this section, officials of the government state their case. The former ambassador of the Union of South Africa to the United States, Wentzel C. du Plessis, offers a defense of apartheid. And the country's minister of external affairs, Eric H. Louw, explains the purposes of the policy. The section closes with the Prime Minister Verwoerd's announcement of the prospective establishment of the first of the separate Bantu states.

APARTHEID UNDERWAY [1]

Shortly after the violent [1960] race riots in South Africa, the minister for foreign affairs announced at a press conference: "South Africa is rapidly returning to normal." This was a surprising statement to read, considering that most areas of the country were still being governed under a state of emergency, that some hundreds of political prisoners of all races were being held incommunicado in jail, that the entire police force and half of the territorial army units of the country were still under arms, that the Security Council of the United Nations had formally condemned South Africa's racial policies, and that the prime minister of the country was seriously ill in the hospital with two bullet wounds in his head. . . .

After the weeks of confusion, the government reasserted its authority in a most unmistakable manner, and with the powers given to it under the state of emergency, was able to check the violence. . . . The South African government has ardent supporters who can be numbered in the millions, and its opponents are largely innocent of the methods of effective political organization, let alone political subversion.

But even so, it is altogether impossible to believe in the permanence of the peace which the government managed to impose by force on that part of the population which remains as hostile to the authorities as ever. What . . . happened in South Africa is not an end but a beginning, and it is difficult to tell now where the solution will lie.

The essential facts of the situation in South Africa are not easy to recapitulate, but any attempt at recapitulation must commence with the statement of some bald figures. There are in South Africa today about 3 million whites, about 12 million blacks, and more than a million people of mixed descent, called Cape Coloureds. There are in addition about half a million Indians.

Division Among the Whites

The white population is divided into two groups: the English-speaking group, which comprises about 40 per cent of the whites;

[1] From "The Atlantic Report: South Africa." *Atlantic Monthly.* 205:14+. Je. '60. Reprinted by permission.

and the Afrikaners, or Boers, who are the descendants of the
original Dutch settlers of the Cape. . . . The Afrikaners . . . now
wield total political power in South Africa, though the power of
mining, industry, and finance is still largely in the hands of the
English-speaking group.

The division between these two communities of whites is
intense and bitter, but it is overshadowed by the far deeper and
more tragic division between black and white. It must be
emphasized, incidentally, that neither the English nor the
Afrikaners are new arrivals: they are overwhelmingly South
African by birth and descent. . . .

The Growing Power of the Blacks

The blacks are a people whose condition ranges from prim-
itively tribal to urbanized professional. In general, it is still true
that most Africans in the Union of South Africa are illiterate,
divided among themselves, and deeply confused by their own
sudden emergence into a highly industrialized and competitive
society. It was only some seventy or eighty years ago that the
gold and diamond mines first began to call upon the labor of
large numbers of Africans, and it was barely twenty years ago
that it was realized how rich a manufacturing country South
Africa could become.

But it is also true that the Africans are, with astonishing
speed, becoming better educated, less confused, and more aware
of their own powers and possibilities. And they are doing this
despite the fact that their absorption in an industrial society
has been managed under the worst social conditions imaginable,
as the hideous slum locations around every South African city
testify. To be fair, it must be added that the per capita income
of the Africans in South Africa is the highest in the entire
continent; but it is precisely because the Africans in South Africa
have the little they have that they are so bitterly aware of all
they do not have, politically and materially. . . .

Government Double Talk

Apartheid has, with good reason, become a word of vilification
and abuse in every country of the world outside South Africa;

but what people outside do not realize is that, however offensive it may be to liberal sentiment to have people of different racial groups who live in the same country forcibly separated from one another, apartheid never can really take place in South Africa.

South Africa is the most modern, most highly industrialized, and wealthiest country in Africa, and its modernity, its industry, and its wealth all depend upon the labor of the blacks in the cities and towns and farms of South Africa. The government of South Africa is as anxious as any government anywhere else in the world to have its country increase in wealth, productivity, and power, and for this reason it never has had and never will have the intention of separating from white South Africa the black workers, out of whose toil the wealth of the country comes.

The members of the government talk of separate but equal development in South Africa, of establishing national homes for the Africans, but this is nothing but the most nonsensical double talk. In its complete divorce from any observable or possible facts, the talk of total separation reveals a dreary imperviousness to reality. . . .

New Obstacles to Freedom

In practice, apartheid has meant to the Africans nothing but repression and servitude, because the government separates only in an area where it can separate without affecting in any way the wealth and comfort of the white inhabitants of the country. African rights in South Africa have always been pitifully few, but even those few rights of self-expression and consultation which the Africans did have have been taken away from them.

Out of a legislature consisting of about 160 white members, the Africans were entitled to elect three white representatives to plead their case; this right has been abolished. Two universities in the country used to admit black and white students on terms of equality; they are no longer permitted to do so. And at the primary and high school levels, all government-supported schools for Africans have been forced to follow a syllabus which has the explicit intention of teaching the Africans only what the government thinks will be useful to them in the place the government has put them.

Africans could hold property in freehold in certain areas; they can no longer do so. A whole series of acts with such resounding titles as the Suppression of Communism Act, the Public Safety Act, the Industrial Conciliation Act, and others have given the government the power to deport African political leaders to remote areas of the country, to smash African trade unions, and to break up African political movements; and these powers have been used copiously. What is true of the Africans is true also of the Coloured and Indian communities, who had until now occupied an intermediate position between white and black.

In addition to these new deprivations and penalties, the disabilities which the Africans had previously suffered from have been given a finer definition, a harsher edge, by the government. Social segregation has always been taken for granted in South Africa by all but a minority of self-conscious liberals among the whites and articulate professional and political leaders among the blacks. But now, under the terms of such acts as the Immorality Act and the Provision of Separate Facilities Act, this social segregation has become official policy, zealously pursued, enforced with incredible punitiveness.

Above all, in discussing this type of long-standing grievance, a place of importance must be given to the recent developments of the systems of influx control and registration, which seek to control the movements of Africans from one part of the country to another, or even from one part of a single magisterial district to another part of that same district.

The pass laws are of a complexity which would require a lawyer to unravel: but any policeman knew that unless an African could produce his reference book, containing, in addition to his tax receipts, a whole series of official entries giving him permission to live where he happens to live and to work where he happens to work, he could be arrested on the spot. In any year, hundreds of thousands of Africans are arrested for pass offenses alone. . . .

What Hope?

The outlook for South Africa is an extremely grim one. If there is any hope at all, it lies in the fact that the government has applied its apartheid measures only in ways which have not affected the wealth and comfort of the white inhabitants of the country. But the wealth and comfort of the whites are now being affected, very deeply, by the ruinous policies which the government is pursuing. . . .

Do the white people of South Africa value sufficiently their own lives and livelihoods to make . . . [changes]? It is difficult to say. There does seem to be a fluidity about white attitudes which has never before been manifest, but little can be expected from those who are at present in power. They are people who dreamed of domination and authority, and though the dream has turned into a nightmare, and though they are now aware that it is a nightmare, they cling to it, more frightened of the common daylight than they are of the horrors they have themselves evoked.

If these leaders waken at all, it will be suddenly; but it may well be that nothing, not even the voice of their own simplest material ambitions, will ever rouse them from their tormented sleep. It is not only the blacks in South Africa whom the world should pity.

THE HUMAN MEANING OF APARTHEID [2]

To come anywhere near understanding apartheid, an outsider must free himself of a misleading impression held by many visitors to South Africa. This is the temptation to equate apartheid with discrimination against the Negro in New York or London.

There is a vast difference between the two. The Negro in America or Britain now has law on his side. He may assert his dignity as a human being with a confidence based on the knowledge that, whatever the racists may do to him, the law is solidly behind him. The reverse obtains in the Republic of South Africa.

South African segregation is backed by the state. . . .

Apartheid or separate development [reads one government statement] is the word that epitomizes the government's policy towards the Bantu: It stands for the separate, orderly and systematic development of the

[2] From article by Nathaniel Nakasa, an African journalist on the staff of *Drum* magazine, published in Johannesburg. New York *Times Magazine*. p 42+. S. 24, '61. Reprinted by permission.

European and Bantu, each in his own respective, geopolitical homeland, each according to his own innate qualities, characteristics and disposition. . . .

Taken to its logical ends, this could mean a state within a state. Within common frontiers we would have a black premier and a white one, a defense force for each, and two independent economies. But, as alarmed whites are forever assured, such a situation will come only in the very remote future. For the time being, apartheid means something else. . . .

The Pass System

In an attempt to separate white communities from black ones, the Africans are controlled by a vast machinery of government documents called passes. Almost the size of a pocket testament, with nearly a hundred pages, the pass bears a photograph of the owner, plus his name and tribe. Also in the book are recorded his employer's name and address.

Without a pass, the African is as vulnerable as a criminal on the run. He is required by law to produce it at any time of the day or night if a policeman wants to see it. . . .

The African who is arrested [for not having his pass] may appear in court on the following day to face the charge of "failing to produce" his pass. "One pound or two weeks," the Bantu commissioner may rule. If he cannot pay his fine, he may be handed to a farmer, who will pay nine pence a day for the man's labor.

In this respect the pass system is the cornerstone of apartheid. While it compels the required number of Africans to accept employment in the cities, it also helps in channeling of African labor to the white farms where wages are poorest.

The pass laws are strictly enforced throughout the Republic. The African is so perilously exposed to danger without a pass that two African men died in a fire in 1959 while trying to rescue their passes from the flames of a burning cosmetic factory.

Apartheid takes other forms. There is, for instance, a permanent curfew in all South African cities. Various buildings bear such notices as "DOGS AND NATIVES NOT ALLOWED" and cinema houses display warnings, "NOT FOR NATIVES AND CHILDREN UNDER 12." Many city parks and libraries are exclusively for whites.

It is amusing to watch white hobos sprawled on seats in the Johannesburg Library gardens where Africans are not allowed.

However distinguished an African may become, there is no hope of escaping his black skin. In fact, outstanding success in business or education often brings increased frustration.

There is the recent case of Louis Nkosi, twenty-three, an African journalist who won a much-coveted Nieman Fellowship to study at Harvard University. Two white journalists from South Africa also won fellowships and traveled to the States. But Nkosi could not leave because the ministry of the interior had not answered his application for a passport. Many African journalists had been denied passports before and Nkosi expected trouble. But he did not expect that he would be refused a passport. Yet, after waiting for many months, that is what happened.

In desperation, Nkosi sought legal advice and was able to get an "exit permit," a sinister document which is made available to citizens who undertake to leave the country and never come back. Should Nkosi return to South Africa, he will be liable to prosecution. All because of his success.

Nkosi was able to survive such absurdities. He fell back on his sense of humor. "This is it," he said at the airport in Johannesburg. "From now on I'm a full-fledged roving journalist." Earlier, however, a promising African student who had been subjected to similar treatment from the ministry of the interior ended up in a mental asylum.

It has been said time and again that the African's greatest defense against apartheid is his sense of humor, the ability to giggle in the face of danger. An African musician has called it "laughing in order to please." Someone else says it is laughing to avoid the spiritual destruction that would come with brooding.

To the African, it seems stupid to legislate against the right of people to move about at night because people every so often need to be out at that time. So anyone who introduces such legislation appears odd, if not mentally unbalanced. Thus the African pictures himself as mentally healthier than his white counterpart. Africans laugh when a huge bus roars past with one white passenger in it because no Africans are allowed to use it.

Apart from learning to laugh, the African has resigned himself to living outside the law, something inevitable in a country whose legislation affects living with one's own parents, drinking, looking for work, sex and other human habits. For the African, life has become adventure in the same fashion that it was for the Elizabethan Englishmen who braved the wild seas to find new areas of life.

City Africans drink in *shebeens* (where liquor is sold illicitly) and ignore the danger of being arrested. That it is a crime to drink no longer matters. Africans have worked out their own moral values.

A young man who cannot find a well-paying job takes any job going and augments his earnings by stealing from the stocks of his employer to sell in the African township. Once a young fellow left his job for another one, although the new job paid less. Asked why he had done this, the boy replied: "There was nothing I could steal in that firm."

As a result of this life, sophisticated city youths go to jail regularly in ever increasing numbers. They return to the lively *shebeens* with obvious pride, boasting nicknames like "Boy Seven Years" or "George Ten Years" or "Jimmy Twelve Years." Going to jail has become similar to a phase of growth in any able-bodied man's life.

However, this type of living has taken its toll. The African townships, usually on the outskirts of the white man's towns, are now infested with crime and violence as African butchers African in a community defying all forms of discipline.

Whether apartheid itself will ever work is a question which is still debated in South Africa. It seems clear that apartheid will never work. So far apartheid has not worked, after more than twelve years of rule by successive Nationalist governments, all legislating for apartheid.

Who will dig the roads if Africans are withdrawn from the cities, where the whites have avoided all forms of manual work, regarding it as something below their status? Who will dig the gold and cut the cane? Who will sweep the streets? It is difficult to imagine South African whites accepting such positions, even in the interests of realizing total separation from the African.

There is also not enough money to pay for apartheid. The country cannot afford to provide two trains on one route when there need be only one for both races. There is not enough money to build two public parks where there need be only one.

Black and white South Africa seem trapped together under a common destiny, in the same country at the same time. The crucial question for the African now is who will help him out of his predicament? Every peaceful form of protest has failed under the formidable military superiority of white South Africa.

THE PASS SYSTEM [3]

Every year in South Africa one out of every seven African men is convicted of an offense against the pass laws. Nearly all of those convicted spend some time in jail, either awaiting trial or because they have not the money for fines. Many thousands more escape court convictions only by paying a fine on admission of guilt. . . .

The pass system has become a focal point of African resentment partly because pass books have indeed become the visible signs of a tyrannical network of control. But the pass inspires particular hatred even more because of its immediate impact on Africans' everyday life.

When Africans talk of the pass laws they mean the provisions contained in a number of acts which require Africans to carry documents. These various documents control every aspect of the African's daily life. Without the right document properly endorsed by a host of authorities, he cannot seek work, live in a town or even walk in its streets.

The first pass law was introduced in 1760. It required slaves moving between urban and rural areas in the Cape to carry passes from their masters. . . . Later the use of the pass was extended and it became the means of enforcing contracts as well as of controlling movement.

Originally intended to identify primitive people, the passes are now used to control all Africans whether they are "primitive" or "civilized." Some Africans—teachers, clergymen, landowners, and others, who have been specially vetted—are today granted exemption certificates. But these are also passes—passes which testify that they are not required to carry passes.

The pass against which the African protests specifically today is what the government prefers to call a "reference book." In it

[3] From "Africans' Revolt Against Pass Laws," by George Clay, Johannesburg correspondent for the *Scotsman*, Edinburgh. *Scotsman*. p 13. My. 26, '60. Reprinted by permission.

all the documents the African has to carry are contained in one cover. This superpass was introduced in 1952.

In spite of their vigorous opposition, which enlisted the sympathetic support of many white women, African women are now being forced to carry these pass books. Soon an African woman will be liable to the same penalties as a man if she is unable to produce her reference book when challenged. For it is not only an offense not to possess a reference book. It is a crime not to have it on one's person.

Effects of the System

Any policeman can demand to see any African's pass at any time of the day or night. Night after night police break into African homes and turn whole families out of bed in the course of pass raids. If a man is picked up without a pass he may be away from work for days without being able to notify his employer or his family. He may lose his wages while he is away —or lose his job altogether.

The pass system has left its mark not only on individuals but on society. . . .

Enforcement of the pass laws [has] meant the creation of a number of technically criminal offenses which bred familiarity with jail and contempt for the law among otherwise law-abiding Africans.

In 1942 the Smit Report pointed out that the country was paying a tremendous price for the pass laws in costly administration and loss of labor during periods of detention. Fines were a drain on the African's meager resources, and constant harassment and interference with the freedom of movement was giving rise to a burning sense of grievance and injustice which had an unsettling effect on the African population as a whole. This committee recommended the abolition of the pass laws. Instead, controls have been increased and the pass laws even more rigidly applied.

APARTHEID IN ACTION [4]

In Education. . . . The policy of apartheid provides the government with complete control of the economic and cultural

[4] From *South Africa and the Rule of Law*, by the International Commission of Jurists. Geneva. '60. p 76-82, 39-45.

status of the nonwhite. Such control has now been taken by the central government from the provinces. . . . Government control . . . commenced with the passage of the Bantu Education Act of 1953. This act was, moreover, not initiated by the minister of education but by the then minister of native affairs, Dr. Verwoerd [now prime minister], who said while introducing the bill:

> Education must train and teach people in accordance with their opportunities in life, according to the sphere in which they live. Good racial relations cannot exist where education is given under the control of people who create wrong expectations on the part of the native himself. . . . Native education should be controlled in such a way that it should be in accord with the policy of the state. . . Racial relations cannot improve if the result of native education is the creation of frustrated people.

It is not difficult to perceive that the Bantu Education Act of 1953, its amendments and subsequent acts pertaining to education are necessary to complement the African reserve, group areas and pass law legislation which aim at separate and restricted development of the nonwhite only to the labor level required by the Europeans. This fact was concisely stated by Dr. Verwoerd again in 1954 when he said that

> the Bantu must be guided to serve his own community in all respects. There is no place for him in the European country above the level of certain forms of labor . . . [and] it is of no avail for him to receive a training which has as its aim absorption in the European community, where he cannot be absorbed. . . .

It is apparent that . . . parents [are deprived] of the essential right to choose freely the kind of education to be given to their children. Further, the introduction into Bantu education of different syllabuses which place greater emphasis upon manual training, may be consistent with the government's economic policy referred to above, but certainly deprives the African of full educational opportunity and development. The Act entrusts wide control and administration of African education to the minister of native affairs. His powers include the appointment and discipline of teachers, and the suspension and expulsion of pupils. . . .

The significance of such complete government control of African education and the results it is intended to produce has perhaps best been summed up by Dr. Verwoerd as follows:

What is the use of teaching the Bantu child mathematics when it cannot use it in practice? That is quite absurd. . . . Education must train and teach people in accordance with their opportunities in life, according to the sphere in which they live. . . . It is therefore necessary that the native education should be controlled in such a way that it should accord with the policy of the state.

Recently as a logical corollary to the above expression of government policy, university education also has been brought within the framework of apartheid legislation. Prior to 1957 the situation was as follows: two "open" Universities of Cape Town and of the Witwatersrand (Johannesburg) admitted both whites and nonwhites on equal academic footing, with attendance at the same lectures and freedom to become members of the same student societies. The Durban branch of the University of Natal admitted nonwhites but maintained segregated lectures and societies. The Pietermaritz branch of the University of Natal admitted only white students, as did also the Afrikaans-speaking Universities of Stellenbosch, Pretoria, the Orange Free State and Potchefstroom. Rhodes University admitted nonwhites as research workers and its affiliate Fort Hare University College was for nonwhites only. In terms of statistics as measured in 1954 the attendance of nonwhites at these institutions was as follows: University of Cape Town, 271; University of Witwatersrand, 214; University of Natal (Durban only), 327; University College of Fort Hare (nonwhites only), 370; University of South Africa (tuition by correspondence only), 1,145.

Even this scant attendance (i.e., 2,327 out of a currently estimated population of 11.5 million nonwhites) existing under the above-mentioned situation soon became an object of concern to the government which desired to complete its policy of total separation. . . .

The government in 1957 introduced the Separate University Education Bill, which was after much protest reentitled and passed in 1959 as the Extension of University Education Act. The Extension of University Education Act effectively removes nonwhites from the Universities of Cape Town and Witwatersrand and the Durban branch of the University of Natal. The removal is completed by providing that as of January 1, 1960, no nonwhite students may register at or attend such universities without the written consent of the minister of Bantu education.

The Act provides for the establishment of three separate colleges for Africans, each according to a particular ethnic group. These are Xhosa College in the Cape, Zulu College in Natal and Sotho Tswana College in the Transvaal, which are to be financed from the Bantu Education Fund. Colleges for Coloureds and Asians are to be established and supported from the general revenue account. Broad, far-reaching powers with respect to the nonwhite colleges are extended to the minister of Bantu education.

In Trade Unions. The rigid distinction between the races which characterizes the labor system of South Africa reveals the true basis of the present policy of apartheid as applied to all spheres of African life. . . .

A century ago the mining and manufacturing industry was almost nonexistent and major labor legislation was passed only when the labor market had already developed. The first act in this field dealt mainly with disputes arising between masters and servants (i.e., domestic servants and agricultural laborers). Towards the end of the nineteenth century the mining industry became more and more important and called for new labor legislation concerning above all two problems: first, a solution had to be found to satisfy the suddenly accelerated demand for skilled and unskilled workers and, secondly, a system had to be established by which immigrating European workers on the one hand, and the large number of rural Africans newly recruited to industry, the imported Indian, Chinese and other Coloured workers on the other, could be kept under control. For this general purpose various laws were enacted such as the Mines and Works Act of 1911, the Labour Regulation Act of the same year, the Workmen's Wages Protection Act of 1914, the Native Urban Areas Act of 1923.

All this legislation as well as its practical implementation is based upon separation of the races: professional, supervisory and skilled work is performed mainly by Europeans, to a lesser extent by Coloureds and Asiatics, while there are almost no Africans in this category. This is true for all branches of economic activity: agriculture, mining, manufacturing, transport, public administration and professional work; exceptions are made only in the fields of teaching and religion where the non-Europeans may serve members of their racial community. Indeed, in 1957, the Nursing Act strongly affected this field as well. The Nursing Act laid down that the Nursing Council, which deals with registration, training and discipline of nurses and midwives, is to consist of white persons only. The Council is to keep separate registers for nurses and midwives of the different races and is empowered to prescribe different qualifications for registration and different uniforms and badges. It provides that except in cases of emergency no white nurse may be employed under the control or supervision of any nonwhite nurse. The restrictions upon Africans taking on skilled jobs in competition with whites can be traced back to the early days of industrialism and was developed mainly in connection with the hiring of labor and conditions of work in the mining industry. Thus the Native Labour Regulation Act and the Mines and Works Act, both of 1911, provided not only for the supervision, control and recruitment of white labor as mentioned above, but also for a graded system of wages and the establishment of native labor bureaus in mines and works. In 1949, the minister of labor was empowered by the Native Law Amendment Act to extend the Native Labour Regulation Act to other industries. . . .

The principle of excluding natives from a specific kind of work was greatly extended in the years following the victory of the Nationalist party in 1948. Under the Native Building Workers Act of 1951, a prohibition was placed on the employment of skilled African building workers in the urban areas. An amendment to this act was passed in 1955 which prohibited the employment of native workers except where the work was on the premises owned and occupied by the native and his dependents or intended for occupation by same.

By the legislation a "bulwark has been set up against the encroachment by Africans on skilled jobs that are regarded as the prerogative of Europeans" [Tom Soper, in *Race Relations Journal*, 25:11, July-December 1958]. The effect has been the establishment of . . . a "multiracial system based on industrial caste" with the result that "no important South African industry is composed of a labor force graded in remuneration, skill, or type of operation, wholly in accordance with the technical requirements or the objective criteria of the worker's productivity" [M. Frankel, *Economic Impact on Underdeveloped Countries*, Oxford, 1953, p 121]. As a result, whites monopolize all supervisory positions irrespective of their personal capacities. Conversely, the African is prevented from obtaining a qualified professional training which would give him the possibility of earning higher wages. The wage problem is, indeed, one of the most serious consequences of the discrimination against African workers, whose wages are considerably lower than those of any other class or group. . . .

These various aspects of racial discrimination in the economic field constitute the primary objective of the policy of apartheid, which is the maintenance of European supremacy in every sphere of life while at the same time promoting the industrial development of the country. The latter cannot be done without the active support of the African workers, who are a major factor in the entire economic system. It may be recalled that today approximately 10 million Africans are spread over the whole country, and provide its basic labor force. At present only some 4 million Africans, most of them women, children and older men, live permanently in the reserves while the balance are employed in the mines, industry, agriculture or as domestic help in urban centers. According to the 1951 census, the African population consisted of approximately 27 per cent urban and 73 per cent rural dwellers. Of the rural population, 53 per cent lived in African territories or reserves, 37 per cent on farms owned by Europeans and 10 per cent in country towns and other rural areas. There is a constant move of Africans into European urban areas, partly as migratory labor but even more as settlers in municipally provided locations or squatters' towns.

The economic necessity of African migration from the reserves, arising out of the industrial development in white areas and excluding in advance the achievement of total apartheid, requires the strictest possible government control over the migratory labor force. This control is most clearly manifest in the restrictions on freedom of movement and residence. . . .

It should be added that South African law recognizes only those trade unions which are registered under the Industrial Conciliation Act. Although there is no explicit legal prohibition preventing the formation of African trade unions, they cannot be registered and therefore are excluded from rights under the latter act. All industrial conciliation measures . . . have in general regarded only Europeans, Coloured and Indians as "employees," with the effect that African trade unions are nonregistrable. The Industrial Conciliation Act of 1956 provided that no further mixed unions (with both white and Coloured membership) would be registered, and after May 7, 1958, any remaining mixed unions must organize branches for the white and Coloured members, hold separate meetings and elect all-white executive committees. The Industrial Conciliation Amendment Act of 1959 added even more restrictions upon the African trade unions. It states that no African may be appointed as a representative of the employees, or as an alternate to such a representative, on an industrial council.

In sum then, the entire economy of the Union of South Africa would seem to operate under an elaborate system of apartheid which deprives the African worker of the opportunity of obtaining higher-paid jobs, virtually eliminates his free choice of work and prevents his equal representation in industrial councils and trade unions.

WHY APARTHEID WILL NOT WORK [5]

All responsible South Africans, whatever their political party, know that the time is rapidly passing in which the whites can maintain a monopoly of power. On the other hand, they are all of them determined, with the exception of a negligible fringe of sentimentalists and fellow-travelers, not to be dominated by the Africans, who in spite of great progress are still in the mass uneducated and undeveloped, and the majority of the Coloureds and Indians share this determination to the full. That does not mean, of course, that it would be justified to resist an African political majority for all time. On the contrary, I have no doubt that an African majority will come eventually, but mere existence, in itself, is not an adequate qualification for a vote in a multiracial state.

The Nationalists have chosen the way of racial separation and it would be quite wrong to think of their apartheid philosophy, in theory anyhow, as either willfully stupid or immoral. It was conceived as a serious attempt to deal with a complicated problem and not intended merely as a cloak for oppression. Partition has, after all, been applied as a last resort in quite a few parts of the world where it has appeared that racial or

[5] From article by Harry Oppenheimer, chairman of the Anglo American Corporation and of the De Beers Consolidated Mines, Ltd. *New Republic.* 144:17-18. F. 20, '61. Reprinted by permission.

communal problems were insoluble within a single state. The Nationalists say that the reserves will be consolidated and energetically developed economically and politically to equip them to govern themselves. It has been made clear by the prime minister of South Africa that while these territories would have to remain for a long and undefined period under the control of the white government of the Union, the ultimate objective is full independence with a right of secession.

Now this is all very well in theory but the practical difficulties in the way are formidable and, to my mind, insuperable. Exhaustive inquiry by a commission which was well-disposed to the government's basic ideas has shown clearly that no conceivable amount of development in the existing reserves would enable them to carry a high enough population to allow a real separation of black and white to take place. It is significant of the political limitations within which the apartheid policy could be applied that no consideration whatever has apparently been given to increasing the size of the reserves so as to divide the area of the Union between black and white on a basis fair to both races.

In the next place, the whole economic development of South Africa has been based on the use of African labor. This labor is partly tribal and migrant, but increasingly it is becoming detribalized and permanently resident outside the reserves. A continuation of this state of affairs is quite incompatible with a genuine policy of separation, but large-scale replacement of Africans by whites in industry is clearly impossible. It would require, to begin with, European immigration on an impracticably large scale and this, anyhow, for other reasons would almost certainly be unacceptable to the Nationalist government. In practice, while very little has so far been done to develop the native areas, a great deal has unfortunately been done to regulate the lives of Africans living outside the reserves on the assumption that effective territorial separation of the races is on the point of being brought about.

The Urban Africans

African residents in the cities are treated as though they were temporary visitors from another country. They are not allowed to own their own houses, have to produce passes on demand and may be forced to leave the urban areas at short notice if they fall out of employment. In this way family life is often broken up and a grave sense of grievance and frustration caused amongst the most developed Africans who should be the leaders of their people.

It is these negative aspects of the apartheid policy which lie behind the disturbances such as took place at Sharpeville . . . [in 1960] and the most urgent need in South Africa is for reform of the laws governing the urban Africans. Dr. Verwoerd has expressed his intention of pressing ahead energetically with positive steps to develop the reserve areas. I would be the last to deny that there is much good in this policy. The economy of the reserves has been neglected and I would agree that, if a larger African population can be enabled to live in these areas and if an effective local self-government can be built up among them, it would help race relations practically and psychologically in the country as a whole. But this, of course, is a very different thing from saying that the whole racial problem can be solved by separation, and eventual partition. It seems to me absolutely certain that it cannot. The experiment on which the government is engaged is, I think, bound to fail and South Africa will have to turn to a policy of unity on a basis of individual merit in the place of division on a basis of race. What would such a policy mean? In the first place it implies that anyone, irrespective of race, who has certain reasonable educational or property qualifications must be entitled to vote on a common roll. It means too that the fear of discriminatory treatment of one race by another must be removed so far as possible by positive guarantees in a rigid constitution which could not be altered without the approval of the racial groups.

What are the chances of such a policy succeeding? I think it is fair to answer that by asking what the chances are of anything else. A stable political system must correspond with the facts of power. That is surely the only way to stability and progress in any country. In South Africa it is more and more clear that the facts of power will not, in the long run, allow government on the basis of domination of one race by another and the facts of economics press more and more in the direction of cooperation and unity.

Throughout Africa we are going through a difficult and testing time and South Africa's policy has for long been the despair of her friends and the comfort of her enemies. Nevertheless it is said, very rightly, in the mining world, that it takes a very bad manager to spoil a good mine, and it is in the Union, more than anywhere else in Africa, that the long-term prospects not only for economic progress, but for racial peace, are best. That is certainly not because South Africans are wiser or better than others, but because the more equal racial distribution and the facts that the African population is accustomed to working with Europeans, is more industrialized, better educated and living on a higher economic level than elsewhere in southern Africa, are all powerful factors making for harmony. It may be that the Union, for so long the problem child in the African family, may lead the way to sanity and peace.

HAVE THE MODERATES A CHANCE? [6]

I agree with much that Mr. Oppenheimer says, but I wish to dissent from any rosy hope expressed in certain government, academic, and even business circles that somehow things will get better if the moderates in South Africa can be encouraged while the extremists are not irritated.

This idea develops from a confused analogy with our South. The defect of this analogy is simple. The South African antagonists are much further apart than those in Louisiana or even Mississippi, and the South African moderates, while they hold similar economic positions to the moderates in Georgia, have far less political power and influence on their community. If they are English-speaking South Africans, and most are, the ruling Afrikaners will disregard them almost completely, and denounce their ideas as a device to destroy the Afrikaner *volk*; if they are industrialists such as Mr. Oppenheimer—from either language group—they will be viewed with deep suspicion because industry, after all, is responsible for the integration of the cities; if the moderates are Afrikaners, they will be denounced and ostracized for opposing the unity of the Afrikaner people. And above all, moderation in South Africa cannot benefit from a shared heritage

[6] From "What Chance Have the Moderates?" by Adam Clymer, a reporter for the Norfolk *Virginia-Pilot*, who has traveled extensively throughout Africa. *New Republic*. 144:18-19. F. 20, '61. Reprinted by permission.

of political equality and due process, a tradition that affects Americans below the Mason-Dixon line. The spirit of the old South African Republic of Paul Kruger is the spirit of the Republic of Verwoerd; its constitution provided for "no equality in either church or state."

Because the moderates are thus isolated from direct influence on the government, and because South African electoral realities make it needless for the Nationalists to conciliate them, any hope that the present regime can be influenced toward the "sanity and peace" to which Mr. Oppenheimer refers without some violent shock seems to me vain. The hope even becomes harmful, for it misleads the South Africans themselves, encouraging them to think they have friends in high places here. Thus recently a Nationalist member of the South African parliament returned from a trip to the United States convinced that the World Bank had told him it would help finance Verwoerd's Bantustans. This sort of thing simply encourages South Africans to keep on believing that outside criticism is the work of the irresponsible and the politically impotent.

Would a Tougher Policy Help?

Polite encouragement having affected the Nationalists not at all, there is the possibility that concerted external pressure might. It is worth a try. To have any hope of success, though, it must have the unmistakable support of the United States, not in the form of support to boycotts—which, because of South Africa's labor laws would starve the Africans whom we want most to help—but simply pressure through ordinary diplomatic channels. One may have "sympathy" for the Union's racial problems, yet tell them that their way of trying to solve these problems has only our contempt, that where apartheid is not dishonest it is impossible, and that it is everywhere unjust.

The opportunities for translating this attitude into specific policy appear limited, I grant. One clear route is to halt the continuous and public diplomatic fraternizing with members of the Union government, the hunting trips, the ambassadorial speeches (widely reported in the press) stressing the bonds of friendship between the two governments. These contacts go far beyond the necessities of protocol, and they are distasteful to the real (African) opposition to Verwoerd. In a country where the opposition is accepted as legitimate and proper, it is possible to be in touch with both sides on this pleasant basis, but in South Africa it is not, and these associations imply a favoritism for the incumbents that is dangerous to American prestige.

The only immediate government-connected aid that the Union receives is through railway loans from the World Bank. But these mean quite a bit to the country's transport plans, and indeed to its Bantustan schemes, and repetition of them should be discouraged by the . . . [Kennedy] Administration in Washington.

One immediate, positive opportunity we have involves the High Commission Territories of Basutoland, Bechuanaland and Swaziland, which the South Africans have occasionally claimed because Basutoland is an enclave and the others adjoin the Union. Basutoland is the most important, because it is surrounded by South Africa, and because it is the most populous and most politically advanced. We can rely on the British to protect these territories against South African threats, but we should prod them a bit to push their development. The South Africans are anxious about political progress in these territories. In fact, political and economic development would make a lie of the South African insistence on the backwardness of its "Bantu," and thus make things that much more difficult for the Nationalists. In Basutoland, for example, the greatest needs are for roads, teachers and agricultural instructors, and while there are considerable problems of terrain and language, a sustained effort would show results in the not too distant future.

Such changes in our policy would not be without adverse consequences. We would not be aiding American investors in South Africa (their interests, while a negligible part of American overseas investment, are significant within the Union). But South Africa would be unlikely to react sharply against American capital already there, for it needs the investment. Further, any long-range American association with the oppression of South African labor harms the United States, and though American firms have been good employers in South Africa, they have still had no choice but to comply with the government's discriminatory and restrictive labor laws.

These suggestions . . . are concerned with how we deal with an intolerable situation in South Africa. . . . We must show our opposition to the racism it both professes and practices wherever we can, not only because we want to be able to influence a subsequent regime, but because anything else is self-betrayal.

THE SOUTH AFRICAN GOVERNMENT'S CASE [7]

It would be a good thing, not only for the friendly intercourse between people but also for the peace of the world, if more discrimination were to be applied in the use of the word "discrimination."

Nowadays, under the impact of well-directed propaganda from both Communist and non-Communist sources, words—even beautiful words such as "love," "peace" and "democracy"—have been so twisted and distorted and even wrenched from their real meanings that the broad mass of the people have become confused and bewildered.

In this mass-produced feeling of bewilderment the word "discrimination" is playing an increasing role. It is often used as a weapon against those who prize the things proven by tradition and who set their standards by the good and the beautiful handed on to them by a Western heritage which, thus far, has withstood the test of the centuries reasonably well. . . .

Men, although spiritually equal, are different from one another and will so remain. Propaganda may and does try to conceal this but it cannot change the fact.

In South Africa's policy of apartheid . . . this fact is recognized. Rarely in the history of the world have so many people, with so many differences between them, been brought together in one community living within the close confines of one national boundary under one system of government.

It is not necessary to go too deeply into the facts because the informed reader knows them. It will be sufficient to point to the following: Five societies have to live with one another—a white society, a Bantu . . . society, a Coloured—mixed blood—society, an Indian society and a Pakistani society. There are still smaller

[7] From " 'Apartheid'—Is It Really Race 'Discrimination'?" by Wentzel C. du Plessis, former ambassador of the Union of South Africa to the United States. *U.S. News & World Report.* 48:138-9. Je. 20, '60. Reprinted from *U.S. News & World Report,* published at Washington.

societies, such as the Malay—Moslem—society, the Griqua society
[a mixture of races in the Griqualand districts of Cape Province],
the Rehoboth society [another racial mixture] in South-West
Africa, plus the Hottentot and Bushman societies, also in that
territory. But these we will pass by for the moment. Otherwise,
the picture gets truly involved. The white and Coloured societies
speak two languages, the Bantu society speaks five main languages
plus about sixty dialects, the Indian and Pakistani societies speak
at least five languages. Each maintains a distinct way of life and,
except for the whites and the Coloureds who share the Western
culture, each way of life flows forth from another and separate
culture. Each society treasures its own way of life and applies to
it its own standards of living—even its own definitions as to
what happiness means and what it does not mean. To take an
extreme example, a Bushman living in the Kalahari will sneer
at the white man's concept of happiness and, in many respects,
rightly so.

All the religions of the world are represented in South Africa
and freely practiced. But the Bantu, torn by the impact which
Christianity has made on their spiritual concepts, have in their
society more than 1,500 religious sects. And only about half of
the Bantu have been "converted." The other half cling to what
they had.

How can a reasonable measure of harmony possibly be created
out of all this diversity? One would be inclined to say that it is
not possible. But there is a way and that is to recognize that
people are not the same and, in this recognition, to apply a policy
based on the principle of differentialism—which is what South
Africa seeks to do, though conscious of human fallibility and
laying no claim to perfection in the incidence of some of the
measures flowing forth from the application of the policy. . . .

I admit, and I do so with regret, that the word "apartheid"
has become unacceptable to the world at large. But that is not
because the concept is wrong; it is because the word has become
twisted and distorted in a process of brainwashing of such scope
and of such viciousness that one can only be filled with a sense
of foreboding as to what else cannot be done to this world in
which we live.

The fact is that the relationship of individual toward individual, family toward family, group toward group and nation

toward nation, rests squarely on the concept of apartheid—that is to say on differentialism and all that it implies. And what it implies is a recognition of the fact that people, in being different from one another, yet share a common humanity but that, in this sharing, the highest human right which any man can have is that based on his own individuality.

It also implies that, if any being claims for himself this right to be himself, he must, because this right is inalienable, also concede it to his fellow man.

The white South African, therefore, does not wish to imitate the Bantu, neither does he wish to force the Bantu to imitate him. He wishes to preserve his own identity, based on his own culture and his own way of life and this he also concedes to the Bantu.

Whatever the Bantu wishes to accept from the white man's way of life he must do voluntarily, but neither is going to allow the other to force him into a common mold. Not all the immense pressure which the world can exercise will accomplish this because, in fact, if it is accomplished it will mean the death of white as well as of Bantu society. The resistance to this will, therefore, come not only from the whites but also from the Bantu, except from those who do not cherish an own identity and who have lost their self-respect.

Misunderstanding in the United Nations

But, so it is said and so the world has been conditioned to believe, apartheid is not differentiation but discrimination. The voting in the United Nations illustrates the extent to which this belief is held and the never-ending preoccupation of its committees with the question of discrimination based on race, color or creed illustrates the misconception of what is discrimination and what is differentiation. To discrimination based on race, color or creed there has now also been added discrimination based on language and sex and so the list of discriminations will steadily grow in the effort to create a pattern of universality for all of humanity and, thereby, a world which, in its drabness, will be a place hardly suitable for human habitation. Perhaps it is just as well that we are beginning to think in terms of removing ourselves to the moon.

Leaving aside, for the moment, the question of discrimination based on religion, the question must be asked: Is it true that differences between people based on race, color, language and sex are discriminatory? It need not be true and by and large it is not true. In the great majority of cases race, color and language, far from being discriminatory, can be identified as the unifying factor in any particular group. They distinguish people from one another and, unless one actually wants this drab universality, it is necessary that people be distinguished from one another, just as the myriad of elements in nature are distinguished from one another and, yet, in the sum total of their diversity form one glorious whole.

I believe that there is much less discrimination in the world because people are of a different race, have a different skin pigmentation or speak a different language than propaganda would have us believe. Leaving aside the sense of frustration which many harbor within themselves and which they alone can remove, it must be clear that what so often appears to be discrimination is only due to the fact that people of the same race, the same color, speaking the same language, through these associations cherish and preserve the same way of life and, consequently, group themselves together in a natural process.

This grouping together, just as naturally, holds within itself an act of exclusion. All of nature does that, but it is this act of exclusion which is now stigmatized as discrimination which, actually, it is not. It is differentiation based on the inescapable fact that people are of different races, *do* have a different color, *do* speak different languages and *do* have different ways of life. Even revolution will not be able to change this and, if brotherhood is to be achieved through such a revolution, it can, indeed, only create an equality of misery under a brotherhood of the revolutionary managers. . . .

It remains important, and will always so remain, to distinguish between discrimination, differentiation, inequality, and, finally, injustice.

If the world . . . wishes to condemn South Africa for inflicting injustice on some of its inhabitants, then that is a matter about which we can argue. Where injustice in fact exists it will be the government's responsibility to see that it be removed. It will, however, be comparatively easy for South Africa to prove that it

has brought about a much higher standard of justice, especially
in the social service and economic fields, than in most parts of
Africa and the hitherto colonially subjugated countries in any
part of the world.

But apartheid *itself* cannot be equated with injustice—it rests
on too sound a basis for that. Anyone condemning it, in fact,
condemns himself because everybody everywhere practices it
every day.

THE PURPOSE OF APARTHEID [8]

What actually is the basis of the charges made against
South Africa, inside and outside of this Assembly?

The white population of South Africa is a permanent one
whose ancestors came to the country more than three hundred
years ago.

The Bantu or black peoples of South Africa are not the
original inhabitants of the country. . . .

South Africa is today the most highly developed and industrialized country in the continent of Africa. This was accomplished against tremendous odds with considerable sacrifices, and
by the initiative of South Africans of European descent.

And now the white population of South Africa is being told
by the Afro-Asian countries, and also by . . . certain Western
countries, that what has been built up over three centuries by
their forebears and successive generations of white South Africans
must be placed under the control of the nonwhite majority.

Would the United States of America, Canada, the Latin
American states—all countries whose respective early histories of
colonization are similar to that of South Africa—would they, if
their relative proportions of white to nonwhite populations were
the same as in South Africa, be prepared to hand over the control
of their countries to Negro or to Indian majorities?

The policy of separate development, also known as apartheid,
is not, as is generally alleged, the evil conception of the present
government, and more particularly the present prime minister,

[8] From address by Eric H. Louw, South Africa's minister of external affairs, before
the United Nations General Assembly, October 11, 1961. Text reprinted from the
New York *Times*. p 8. O. 12, '61.

Dr. Verwoerd. It is a policy which is equally in the interests of the white and the Bantu population. It is intended to safeguard what has been built up over three centuries by the whites, but at the same time it takes account of the political aspirations, as well as of the traditions, cultures, and also the material needs of the Bantu peoples.

The Bantu Self-Government Act provides for progressively increased legislative, judicial and administrative powers for the Bantu authorities in their territories. These territories, mostly situated in the most fertile areas of South Africa, were voluntarily occupied by the Bantu tribes, which at the time of the arrival of the first Dutch immigrants, were themselves migrating from Central and East Africa. The territories were subsequently reserved for the Bantu only.

Under this system of self-government the Bantu have since 1951 increased their governing councils from about 60, with about 300 individual members, to 445 councils with no fewer than 6,550 individual members in 1961. This shows that the system is not only democratic but that it has been well received by the Bantu, in spite of attempts by subversive organizations and white agitators to discredit this policy and to create unrest.

South Africa's policy is not, as is sometimes alleged one of "back to the tribe," or "back to the bush." The object is to start with a system of government which is based on Bantu custom and tradition, but which will be further developed by the progressive introduction of fully representative government.

The leaders of Bantu territorial authorities have in public statements signified their unqualified acceptance of the government's policy of separate development and have also expressed their appreciation of what is being done to develop self-government in the different Bantu ethnic areas.

I would add here that in order to accelerate the transfer of administrative and judicial functions to the recognized leaders of the Bantus, special schools have been and are in the process of being established in the different ethnic areas for the training of young men who are likely to be leaders of their people in modern methods of administration and also in economic and business principles.

There are 2.5 million Bantus who work and live in the European urban areas. Another 3 million are scattered in other

European areas. It has been urged here, and elsewhere, that they should receive full political equality with the whites. I have already explained that the Bantu who live in the white areas will retain their voting rights in the self-governing areas from which they come and can return there for that purpose, as is done by many of the 400,000 Bantu from the neighboring British protectorate of Basutoland who are working in the Republic.

The great progress made in Bantu education in South Africa is considerably in advance of that made by most other African countries. . . .

By contrast [to other areas of Africa], there is peace, prosperity and economic stability in South Africa, in spite of attempts by agitators and subversive elements, inside and outside of South Africa, to stir up trouble among the nonwhites and to harm South Africa's economy.

Inside South Africa there are subversive Bantu organizations, aided and abetted by overseas ultra-liberalistic organizations, such as the American Committee on Africa in New York and Christian Action in London and by certain sections of the press in those countries.

We firmly believe that the course upon which we have embarked in South Africa will ultimately solve the problem of relations between white and nonwhite races in our country. It is a policy which aims at progressively giving to the Bantu the complete control of his own homelands, and which by means of urban councils, will provide the urban Bantu with the means to promote their material welfare and social needs. Similar steps have been taken, and will be further developed also in the cases of the Coloured and Indian population.

All that we ask is that we be permitted to carry out our policy of looking after the interests of our Bantu and other nonwhite peoples without interference from outside, be it from Western, Eastern or African countries.

THE FIRST BANTU STATE:
THE PRIME MINISTER'S ANNOUNCEMENT [9]

[On January 23, 1962, Prime Minister Hendrik F. Verwoerd unexpectedly announced that one of South Africa's largest non-

[9] From "First Bantu State Established Within South Africa," advertisement submitted by the Information Service of South Africa, 655 Madison Ave., N.Y. and printed by the New York *Times*. p 17. Ja. 24, '62.

white areas (on the southeast coast) would be granted internal self-government early in 1963. This was in pursuit of the policy of apartheid which envisages the separate and even independent development of African states apart from the white population of the new Republic. For a generation, it was intimated, such states would be under the tutelage of the Republic, since foreign affairs, defense, and justice would be dealt with by the present government of South Africa. Matters regarding agriculture, health and welfare services, lands, roads, education, and local authority would become the responsibility of the new state.

The plan has been greeted with opposition partly because the announcement was unexpected and partly because the Xhosa, who inhabit the area, are also spread through other parts of the Republic. Inasmuch as it is such a new venture and may be repeated in as many as two hundred or more smaller areas, it is important to consider the official view of the government. The statement which follows was issued by the South African Information Service in New York and includes a summary of the announcement made by Dr. Verwoerd—Ed.]

A decisive step was taken this week with the establishment of a new Bantu state to solve the complex population problems facing the Republic of South Africa.

The Transkei, traditional homeland of the Xhosa peoples, became the first Bantu territory within the borders of the Republic of South Africa to receive self-government under a democratic constitution. Prime Minister Verwoerd announced that the Transkei will get effective self-rule through an elected parliament and under a new constitution which will begin to operate in the first half of 1963.

Self-government for the various Bantu nations in the territories to which they have the inalienable right of occupation, is the cornerstone of the South African government's policy of national reconstruction.

The announcement that follows is necessary for a better understanding of objectives about which there has been much misunderstanding over the years. It is presented as a public service by the Information Service of South Africa for the benefit of readers to whom it may not otherwise be available in such detail.

The prime minister of the Republic of South Africa, Dr. H. F. Verwoerd, in summarizing his announcement in parliament in

Cape Town said: "I have just announced in parliament details of the granting of self-government to the Transkei.

"The Transkei is the first Bantu homeland which has approached the government of the Republic to aid it, by means of this great step on the road to independence, for which in its final form it rightly feels it is not yet ready. My government is prepared to grant the Transkei a new constitution which will create a parliament and a cabinet of ministers based on the principles of Western democracy.

Parliament and Franchise

"The details of the constitution will be worked out in consultation with the Bantu leaders of the Transkei. This will include the constitution of its parliament and the exercise of the franchise.

"The Transkei will have a wholly black parliament and cabinet, since the white inhabitants of the Transkei will have no political rights there but in the Republic. A separate Transkei citizenship for the Bantu will be granted and details will be worked out how, at this stage of development, this may be coupled with the advantages of South African citizenship.

Transfer of Power

"The powers entrusted to the new parliament will be substantial and will increase. Presumably control over agriculture, education and welfare services, lands, roads, local affairs, etc., will be placed under Bantu jurisdiction forthwith. External affairs, defense and certain aspects of the administration of justice *inter alia* will presumably for the time being remain the responsibility of the Republic.

"It is hoped that consultation on the constitution will be completed in time to have the new system in operation during the first half of 1963. For the civil service of the new government, white officials will be made available in order to train the Bantu as rapidly as possible to fill these posts. A five-year replacement program of as many white civil servants as possible by Bantu will be worked out by the department of Bantu administration in conjunction with the new Transkei government.

Economic Aid

"In order to get the new administration in sound financial trim, the republican government will divert the income from all direct taxation hereto obtained from the Transkei Bantu, both within and without the territory, to its use. The republican government will also make an annual grant, equivalent to the expenditure of the departments concerned and the Bantu Trust in connection with those tasks to be taken over now, in order to enable the Transkei parliament to function adequately. In addition, more funds will be made available to meet additional expenses which the new situation will require.

"Political development must naturally be accompanied by economic development on a substantial scale. The planning includes a five-year program by the department of Bantu administration, Bantu Trust and the Transkei government; economic aid through the Bantu Finance Corporation; the establishment of a development corporation for the Transkei and a five-year program for the development of border industries. White initiative and know-how will be provided by private enterprise without being exploited by the creation of private white vested interests within these areas.

Example for Others

"What has been announced for the Transkei serves as an example of how the republican government will fully implement its policy of separate development for each of the other Bantu nations as soon as they feel capable or desirous of making such a request.

"The black man, as a member of one or other of the existing Bantu nations, is intent, just like the white South African, upon safeguarding his national heritage. Whilst fully appreciative of the necessity to adjust Bantu society to the prerequisites of modern statehood, their wiser leaders will not countenance any development which threatens their own existence as separate nations.

"The South African government has chosen the only alternative to the creation of a multiracial state, namely the self-realization to the utmost extent possible for each group. This means that the government is willing to grant to the Bantu nations of South Africa the opportunity to work out their own destinies just like all other new states in other parts of Africa and Asia.

"An enormous program for the development of political self-realization of each national group is therefore being devised. The support already obtained for this program gives the lie to the propaganda that there is a widening chasm between whites and nonwhites in South Africa.

"Despite provocation, criticism, and extremist demands, the republican government is determined to solve the political problems of the country and its peoples in such a way that stability and tranquillity for all is assured. In contrast to the chaos and turbulence elsewhere in Africa, the South African government has refused to allow itself to be provoked to undertake extreme measures in its primary and legitimate function of ensuring law and order.

"The new South Africa, which is being constructed by the measures announced today, holds within it great promise for the building up of friendship and cooperation between the races. It furthermore guarantees to each the retention of his own identity. All the nations of the world which seek to protect human dignity and the right to self-determination should give South Africa a fair chance to establish and develop its own commonwealth of nations."

III. POLITICS AND OPINION IN
SOUTH AFRICA

EDITOR'S INTRODUCTION

The diversity of opinion in South Africa finds various outlets—
through party contests, underground movements, church circles
—despite government attempts to suppress the views of those
opposed to the principle of apartheid. Novelists and other members of the intelligentsia have questioned the government's present
course. There has also been much soul-searching within the
Afrikaner religious community about apartheid, and businessmen,
who realize so clearly that the economy rests on cooperation of
the races, are concerned. Even outright Communist propaganda is
found in South Africa. In this section the chief ideas in the
political arena are noted.

The first article is an account of the tragic Sharpeville shooting in 1960, drawn from a report in *Time* magazine. The two
succeeding articles discuss the recent election and its results.
More detailed political party programs and a discussion of the
outstanding extraparliamentary groups (some now underground)
are given by a *Christian Science Monitor* correspondent, John
Hughes. That both white and African groups are in a period of
"rethinking" is indicated by Gwendolen M. Carter, an American
student of South Africa and one of its leading historians. A short
biographical note on Albert Luthuli, winner of the 1960 Nobel
Peace Prize, follows. A news story on a churchman who has
apparently overstepped the bounds of antigovernment criticism
and also the story of Indians in South Africa are reported by a
New York *Times* correspondent, Leonard Ingalls.

In "A Trial and Its Meaning," the celebrated mass treason
trial, begun in 1956 and concluded abruptly in March 1961, is
explained by Thomas G. Karis, a former American Foreign Service Officer, who sheds much light on opinion in South Africa, on
the nature of the government's attempts to stamp out opposition,
and on the probable political consequences of immobilizing so
many opponents of apartheid in recent years. Next a Canadian

Negro who traveled in South Africa reports on his impressions and contacts, some of which foretell violence. The possibility of violent upheaval is also the subject of an article by a correspondent of London's *Observer*.

In the last article Anthony Delius, a staff correspondent of a South African newspaper, predicts a more settled future for all groups in South Africa now in the throes of discovering a common nationhood.

THE SHARPEVILLE TRAGEDY [1]

For years the Africans hated and endured the [pass] system. Then [in May 1960] a new and more militant organization called the Pan-African Congress decided to exploit the passbook grievance. It urged Africans all over the Union to descend . . . upon local police stations—without their passbooks, without arms, without violence—and demand to be arrested. In a few spots, the turnout was impressive. At Orlando township in the outskirts of Johannesburg, twenty thousand Africans milled around the police station, led by Robert Mangaliso Sobukwe, thirty-six, a Methodist-reared university instructor, who heads the Pan-African Congress. Fifteen miles to the south, in Evaton, seventy thousand Africans turned out. The nervous police made few arrests of the demonstrators; at Langa, near Cape Town, they opened fire to disperse the Africans, killing three and wounding twenty-five.

At first, everything was relatively quiet, too, at the Sharpeville police station, twenty-eight miles southwest of Johannesburg—but Sharpeville was soon to become a headline name the world over. Twenty police, nervously eying a growing mob of twenty thousand Africans demanding to be arrested, barricaded themselves behind a four-foot wire-mesh fence surrounding the police station. The crowd's mood was ugly, and 130 police reinforcements, supported by four Saracen armored cars, were rushed in. Sabre jets and Harvard Trainers zoomed within a hundred feet of the ground, buzzing the crowd in an attempt to scatter it. The Africans responded by hurling stones, which rattled harmlessly off the armored cars and into the police compound, striking three policemen.

[1] From "South Africa." *Time*. 75:18-19. Ap. 4, '60. Courtesy *Time*, the Weekly News Magazine; copyright Time Inc. 1960.

Chain Reaction

At 1:20 P.M. the blowup came. When police tried to seize an African at the gate to the compound, there was a scuffle and the crowd advanced toward the fence. Police Commander G. D. Pienaar rapped out an order to his men to load. Within minutes, almost in a chain reaction, the police began firing with revolvers, rifles, Sten guns. A woman shopper patronizing a fruit stand at the edge of the crowd was shot dead. A ten-year-old boy toppled. Crazily, the unarmed crowd stampeded to safety as more shots rang out, leaving behind hundreds lying dead or wounded—many of them shot in the back. It was all over in two awful minutes.

As the police emerged to clean up the carnage, one officer grew sick at the sight and vomited. But the police commander said coolly: "My car was struck by a stone. If they do these things, they must learn their lesson the hard way." The dead—estimates range from seventy-two to ninety—were carted off to makeshift morgues; more than two hundred wounded overflowed the native hospital. And so much plasma was needed that African blood gave out, and the wounded got transfusions from reserve white stocks.

All South Africa was stunned by the sudden bloodshed that had always been implicit in Verwoerd's unrelenting policies. The English-language Johannesburg *Star* assailed the government's "pathetic faith in the power of machine guns to settle basic human problems," and the Anglican Bishop of Johannesburg appealed "to all those in South Africa who have any human feelings" to stop the police tactics. More than five hundred white students at the University of Natal, carrying banners reading HITLER 1939, VERWOERD 1960, assembled on campus to lower the British and South African flags to half-mast.

But in the rest of Africa and throughout the world, the reaction was even angrier. Liberia's President William Tubman called the Sharpeville massacre "the vilest, most reckless and unconscionable action in history." In London, a crowd shouting "Murder!" had to be dispersed from South Africa House under an ordinance that prohibits any public gathering within a mile of Parliament when the House of Commons is in session. In Vatican City, *L'Osservatore Romano* demanded to know why South Africa's police "did not employ such modern means as water hoses and tear gas, which are in use in all civilized countries," instead of mowing down men, women and children indiscriminately. Nowhere in the world did a single government side with South Africa.

Everywhere Deplored

The United States State Department, freely intruding in another nation's internal affairs contrary to usual practice, "deplored" the violence and "regretted" the tragic loss of life. UN Secretary-General Dag Hammarskjold said that the UN was entitled to discuss the race riots, even if it could not intervene over them, and added: "In humanitarian terms, you need not have any doubt about my feelings." On petition of twenty-nine Afro-Asian UN members . . . [a meeting of] the Security Council [was set]. . . .

Even South Africa's rabidly nationalistic Afrikaans press was having second thoughts. The day before the riots, the Johannesburg *Vaderland* called for a "simpler and less hurtful pass system." The influential Cape Town *Die Burger* urged moderation on Prime Minister Verwoerd. But Verwoerd obstinately said that "nothing would be done" to abolish the pass laws, and belatedly discovered that the demonstrators at Sharpeville had "shot first," even though no one found arms on the Africans.

Mourning Day

Afraid of civil war and preparing for a showdown, the government canceled all leaves for the twenty thousand members of the South African police, placed the members of auxiliary white defense forces on a stand-by alert. Indoor or outdoor meetings of more than twelve persons were declared illegal (exception: a political rally of forty thousand addressed by Prime Minister Verwoerd, who complained that most of the unanimous outside criticism came from "the ducktails of the political world . . . . Good and nice people are mostly quiet"). African political organizations were outlawed. Robert Sobukwe and eleven of his Pan-African aides surrendered and were jailed. Albert Luthuli, leader of the more moderate African National Congress, was already under house arrest. Both organizations proclaimed a "day of mourning" for the dead (the police released the bodies a few at a time so that there could be no mass funeral). A work boycott by Africans was ordered, and strong-arm squads called "the Spoilers" walked the streets to keep Africans off the job. Cape Town docks, loading twenty ships, were crippled by a walkout of stevedores. On the Johannesburg exchange, gold stocks fell for a paper loss of $250 million in four days. Throngs of white South Africans, fearing disaster, lined up for emigration data at the information offices of Canada and Australia.

At week's end came the first giving of ground. South Africa's commissioner of police curtly announced that to relieve the "tremendous tension," police would no longer ask Africans to show—or arrest them for failure to carry—the hated passbooks. It represented the first major retreat by the government since the Nationalists won power at the polls twelve years ago. But just when everyone was about to credit Verwoerd's administration with coming to its senses, Defense Minister François Erasmus said that the police decision was "strictly temporary" until the "situation quieted." South Africa's course was still set for disaster.

SOUTH AFRICA FACES THE FUTURE [2]

The Republic of South Africa came into being on . . . [May 31, 1961], and although no general election was due until 1963 it was widely predicted that the Nationalist government would seek fresh electoral endorsement at an earlier date. It did not, therefore, come as a surprise when Dr. Verwoerd announced that elections would be held on 18 October, giving as his reason the need that "all should know a strong and stable government is in power for the next five years."

Dr. Verwoerd stood to gain much from an immediate test of opinion and to lose more by delay. No doubt one of the most important considerations was the economic situation, for there was no guarantee that it would not worsen as the full effects of South Africa's withdrawal from the Commonwealth made themselves felt. . . . There was still a great deal of bewilderment that South Africa had severed the Commonwealth connection and also a fairly widespread willingness among the white electorate to believe there was some substance in the prime minister's assertion that there was no room for white people in an "Afro-Asian domi-

[2] From an article in *World Today*. 17:538-46. D. '61. Reprinted by permission.

nated Commonwealth." The feeling that South Africa stood alone in the world, and the fear that South African society might fall victim to a chain of events such as the Congo had experienced, lent support to the belief that whites in South Africa, for their own salvation, must close their ranks against the "black danger." . . .

The official opposition party (United party) had been showing signs of increasing ineffectiveness and its policy of watered-down nationalism was unlikely to attract new voters or to hold all the old ones. Dr. Verwoerd could therefore hope for some accession of support from United party supporters—particularly those who had voted in favor of the Republic in the 1960 referendum. The results of the general election which showed a pronounced swing towards the Nationalists . . . confirmed this forecast, and the eighteen-year-olds, voting for the first time in a parliamentary election, must also have helped to build up the Nationalist majority. The United party's failure to retain rural support was reflected in the loss of its last country seat (Queenstown). The composition of the new House of Assembly is as follows: National party 105; United party 49; Progressive party 1; National Union 1.

The prospect of reducing the United party's effectiveness still further must have been attractive to Dr. Verwoerd. Of much more significance, however, was the chance to eliminate from the House of Assembly the lively Progressive party—represented by a group of MP's who prior to their breakaway from the United party in 1959 had been among its ablest parliamentarians, and who, since their new Progressive party was founded, had taken the lead in offering vigorous opposition to the government both inside and outside the House. In this aim Dr. Verwoerd's success has not been quite as complete as he would wish, for although the strength of the Progressive party in parliament is now reduced from eleven to one . . . several other Progressive candidates made a very good showing and the measure of support for the party as a whole, particularly in the Johannesburg area and in Natal, was notable.

The Progressive party stands for a much more liberal approach to the race problem than the United party, and it has obviously attracted most of the liberal wing of the United party in a manner which the now almost nonexistent Liberal party was never able to do. With its powerful financial backing and considerable popular support, it is reasonable to think that in time the Progressives will win over new adherents, but from the point of view of the Nationalist government it is clear that the main nuisance of parliamentary opposition has been silenced, and whatever new supporters the Progressive party may win are probably likely to be more than balanced by further defections from the right wing of the United party to the Nationalist camp. Nor does the Nationalist record give ground for optimism that an extraparliamentary group—even when it represents some 100,000 voters—will be able to influence the course of government policy to any marked extent. . . .

It is clear that Dr. Verwoerd intends to deal severely with any symptoms of deviation within the ranks of his own party. His intentions in this respect were made plain at the beginning of . . . [1961] after there had been much discussion in the Nationalist press and among Nationalist supporters about the implementation of apartheid in respect of the Coloured people. In a statement issued by the Federal Council of the Nationalist party . . . [in January 1961], policy towards the nonwhites as a whole, and towards the Coloured people in particular, was reiterated, and any criticisms or digressions from this policy were condemned as disloyalty except where they were put forward at party congresses and officially endorsed there. In order that there should be no misunderstandings about the extent to which official party policy covered controversial issues, not only was the theory of separate development . . . set out, but it was further stated that the Federal Council was convinced that the government was "in a better position to judge" on such matters as consultations with leaders of different racial groups; mixed marriages; migratory labor; job reservation; development of Bantu areas; voting rights for nonwhites; the maintenance of law and order "in the midst of communistic and other incitement" by the use of the judiciary or by stronger means; policy towards Asiatics; protection by the state of groups or churches; etc. Criticism of the government by Nationalists would obviously not be tolerated in the future.

The conflict of conscience which led to representatives of the Nederduitse Gereformeerde Kerk (NGK) associating themselves with the antiapartheid declaration which followed the Consultation with the World Council of Churches held at Cottesloe

(Johannesburg) in December 1960 prompted a further pronounce-
ment in the Federal Council's statement that "all churches have
not yet taken decisions in this matter," followed by a homily on
the moral defensibility of apartheid. The Consultation between
representatives of the World Council of Churches and its eight
member-churches in South Africa was organized after much difficulty, on the original initiative of the Anglican Archbishop of
Cape Town, to seek reconciliation between the South African
churches on the question of racial segregation which had been declared contrary to the Gospel by the World Council of Churches
in 1954, and which the Archbishop of Cape Town maintained
was being identified by Africans with the Christian Church. Two
Dutch Reformed Churches left the World Council of Churches
early this year, having failed to subscribe to the Cottesloe Declaration. Recently, two events would seem to indicate that Dr.
Verwoerd has succeeded in regaining united Church support: the
NGK, like the other two Dutch Reformed Churches, has now left
the World Council of Churches, and Professor A. S. Geyser of
Pretoria University is being tried for heresy as a result of students'
accusations that he questioned the morality of the apartheid
doctrine [see "A Churchman on Trial," in this section, below].

With a majority in the new House of Assembly which falls
short of two-thirds by only one seat and the prospect of scanty
effective opposition, and with apparent victory over dissident
groups in his own party, Dr. Verwoerd can now rule the Republic
from strength. The appointment of two English-speaking cabinet
ministers, Mr. A. Trollip (former Administrator of Natal) and
Mr. Frank Waring—both at one time United party MP's—
fulfills a pre-election promise that if right-wing English-speaking
South Africans supported him he would give them more say in
the government. His aim is obviously to move the Republic out
of the arena of English-Afrikaner political conflict and bring
about a bipartisan white attiude towards racial problems with
the defenses of white interests as its guiding principle. In other
words, among the white South African population, with the exception of Liberal and Progressive elements, we can expect to see
an extension of the *laager* [stockade] mentality which has for so
long been characteristic of the Afrikaner's political outlook.

To meet the danger of civil disorder the South African defense forces are to be reorganized and reequipped with French

and Belgian arms, and all white citizens are being encouraged to learn how to handle weapons. . . .

While the white population prepares to face an uncertain future, there have been few signs that the banned African political organizations have begun to recover from the failure of the various passive resistance movements. The much advertised stay-at-home strike which was planned to take place on Republic Day was largely unsuccessful, and no further national demonstrations have been heard of. There is little doubt that this can be attributed to the difficulties of "underground" planning, to effective police activity, and to the clear indication by the government that it will use the utmost force to suppress any expressions of dissatisfaction. The question must now be asked whether this kind of repression will, in time, provoke a reaction against the policies of nonviolence advocated by leaders of the stature of Mr. Luthuli [see "A Nobel Peace Award Speech,"in Section IV, below], and a recourse to violence by nonwhites. The continuation of the state of emergency in Pondoland and recent reports of widespread arrests of "criminal elements" in all parts of South Africa suggest that the authorities are taking no chances on this score.

The marked upsurge of political consciousness among the Coloured population in recent months is probably likely to have as little effect on the South African government as any other internal or external criticism has done. What of the economic outlook for the Republic? . . .

Economic Aspects

Dr. Verwoerd and members of his government have often proclaimed that their policies will be pursued regardless of economic or other sacrifice, and during the next five years there may well be an intensification of economic difficulty leading to the situation where the South African economy is in a virtual state of siege. According to the governor of the South African Reserve Bank, "certain branches of economic activity have already shown a decline," and his optimism that this tendency will be reversed may not be widely shared. The brunt of a general recession would be carried in the financial, mining, and industrial spheres by urban and largely antigovernment sectors, but the farming community also stands to lose considerably when South African products cease to enjoy preferential treatment in the British market. . . .

Ultimately, of course, a general recession would affect the whole economy. It may be possible to keep white unemployment within reasonable bounds by excluding nonwhites from urban areas and by job reservation—i.e., the reserving of specific jobs for whites—and thus forcing the nonwhite labor force to carry the burden of unemployment. This would have the dangerous corollary that men who are out of work, and near starving, would have little to lose in promoting civil disorder. Up till now, one of the main influences militating against prolonged strikes or stay-at-home demonstrations among the nonwhite population has been their lack of financial and food resources. . . .

Whether it will be possible to sustain a "siege economy" indefinitely remains to be seen. The present external payments situation can, no doubt, be maintained through the retention of strict control and through the careful husbanding of the earnings of gold and of South Africa's other basic exports: it is probably also hoped that the new import restrictions will divert demand to local suppliers and thus offset any recessionary conditions already developing, although higher prices may be necessary to support marginal firms. The authorities on their part will give the economy all the support they can. For example, increased government expenditure is planned to offset a serious fall-off in private building activity reflected in the fact that the value of building plans passed during the first eight months of this year was £13.1 million less than in the corresponding period last year and only amounted to £30.3 million. But this will place heavy burdens on the exchequer which is already faced with substantial outlays for defense and for the implementation of apartheid.

The prospect of an economic standstill not only destroys the hope of an increase in the meager living standard of the Republic's nonwhites but also threatens a gradual lowering of all existing living standards. The prime minister, in a statement issued after a recent meeting of his Economic Advisory Council, admitted that the present tempo of expansion and development in the country is not sufficient to "absorb completely the increasing annual addition to the population."

If the Nationalist leaders have consciously considered the sacrifices which their policies have obliged South Africans of all races to make, and a majority of the white electorate have understood and have consequently seen fit to endorse their actions, then apartheid can only be considered as a reflection of the extent of the racial fears and irrational prejudices which now grip the bulk of the white community. One has to take into account not only actual loss but also the sacrifice of potential gain which has been the price of South Africa's thirteen-year pursuit of this ideal of apartheid. What lies ahead cannot be prophesied with certainty, but one can scarcely be optimistic about the further consequences of policies which have already caused South Africa to forfeit such material benefits as capital, skill, and markets; which have prevented her from making the best use of her own resources; and which have resulted in a disastrous loss of friendship, prestige, and respect in the rest of the world.

AFTER THE ELECTION [3]

In the shadow of Paul Kruger's statue in Church Square, Pretoria, on October 18 [1961], the minister of Bantu administration and development, Mr. M. D. C. de Wet Nel, welcomed the National party's triumph in that day's general elections with these words:

The United Nations knows where it stands and what to expect from my people in this southern corner of Africa. We will die—each and every one of us, every son and daughter of South Africa—rather than give up our nationhood.

The [election] results show that this kind of rabble-rousing appeals to an increasing number of white South Africans. Dr. Verwoerd's National party increased its share of the poll in every seat it contested. It captured three seats from the opposition: two from the United party, the third from the National Union, which had formed a pact with the United party and which failed lamentably to serve as a decoy for dissatisfied Afrikaner Nationalists. The Nationalists now hold 105 of the 160 seats in the all-white parliament—only two short of that cherished South African political ideal, the two-thirds majority. Dr. Verwoerd has a clear mandate from the whites—the wishes of the nonwhite majority are not considered—to push ahead with his separate development

[3] From "Dr. Verwoerd's Mandate," report by an unnamed correspondent in South Africa. Economist. 201:358. O. 28, '61. Reprinted by permission.

policy, which seeks to divide the country into a white parent state
and several black satellite Bantustans. He has five years to make
separate development a reality, no matter what the cost.

But the going will not be easy: the election campaign showed
that the Nationalists are still the prisoners of their own past
propaganda about the "black menace." The rank-and-file Nationalists are more than unwilling to make the economic sacrifices
necessary if genuine Bantustans are to be built up; they are by
nature suspicious of "doing too much for the *Kaffir.*" In a broad-
cast on October 20, Dr. Verwoerd stressed that there will be no
sudden speed-up of separate development. A student of applied
psychology, he understands well the mood of most white South
Africans. . . . [See "The First Bantu State: The Prime Minister's
Announcement," in Section II, above.]

The other feature of the elections was the support gained by
the liberal Progressive party, which the Nationalists had hoped
would be wiped out by the United party. The Progressives won
only one seat from the United party, but they came close to
taking several others. They polled 56,000 votes to the United
party's 83,000 in sixteen urban English-speaking constituencies.
Tens of thousands of people in the cities are apparently prepared
to reject race discrimination—the very basis of South African
political thinking—and to strike out boldly for a shared society
in which individual merit, and not race, will be the criterion. A
heavy burden will rest on the shoulders of Mrs. Helen Suzman,
the only Progressive who won a seat. She will have to carry the
banner in parliament not only of twelve thousand affluent white
voters in Houghton (Johannesburg), but of 10 million nonwhites.
Judging by her performance in parliament during the Sharpeville
emergency last year, she is well qualified for the task. Liberal-
minded people hope that she will become a substitute for Mrs.
Margaret Ballinger, who served as a representative of African
interests in parliament for many years before the Africans' representatives were barred from parliament by Nationalist legislation
in 1959.

Ex-Chief Albert Luthuli, who is also ex-president of the
banned African National Congress, commented in the peaceful
spirit that . . . won him the Nobel Prize. He said he "deeply
regretted" that white voters had given Dr. Verwoerd's party increased support, which amounted to a mandate to continue its

repressive policies. This meant that there would be hard times ahead for South Africa. But characteristically, Mr. Luthuli added that the support which the Progressives had received was an encouraging sign. Although he did not agree totally with the policies of the Progressive party, it was moving along the only true path to healthy race relations in South Africa.

Now that the elections are over, white South Africans are wondering whether the United party, the traditional opposition which has "White Leadership With Justice" as its slogan, has a future. In every election since 1948 it has lost ground; since the death of General Smuts it has lacked not only a leader, but a positive policy. Instead of opposing the Nationalists on principle, it has adopted an expedient "me too" approach: when Dr. Verwoerd came forward with his Bantustan plan, the United party's answer was a vague "race federation" scheme. The party has not accepted what General Smuts would surely have acknowledged— that there is now a clear-cut division between liberal and conservative thought in South Africa. Although the United party won forty-two seats, it lost ground to the left and to the right in every seat contested.

The tide is running strongly in favor of white nationalism in all but a few progressive urban areas; this will surely—and dangerously—stir the embers of nonwhite nationalism. On the eve of the elections, power lines near Johannesburg were sabotaged, and slogans—"The People Shall Govern"—were daubed on an Afrikaans church and on public buildings. This action, it is said, was directed from London. The Nationalist leaders assume that it will be from abroad—from the United Nations especially—that South Africa will be attacked during the coming years of Dr. Verwoerd's rule.

THE FORCES AT WORK [4]

Despite the fog of propaganda, of attack and counterattack, of distortion and untruth, which surrounds so many aspects of South African life today, the truth of the matter is that the average South African longs for peace; he yearns for a quiet and just settlement of his nation's difficulties, and he is neither a

[4] From "South Africa Searches," by John Hughes, staff correspondent of the *Christian Science Monitor*. *Christian Science Monitor*. sec 2, p 9. Jl. 21, '61. Reprinted by permission.

wild-eyed radical, feudal taskmaster, nor a callous and indifferent Christian.

Many onlookers believe that South Africa is today trapped in the biggest single problem facing any nation on earth. They understand the aspiration of the blacks and the fears of the whites. They also recognize that there is no simple, overnight, off-the-cuff solution to this problem.

While no such solution has yet appeared—or seems to be in sight—this does not mean that the many men of good will in this country will not continue searching for an answer to the race question which will be fair to all concerned.

It is true that there are whites whose thinking is not yet abreast of the twentieth century. It is equally true that there are nonwhite leaders who are unrealistic in their demands.

Yet in between these two unhappy extremes are the vast bulk of South Africans of all races who do not want to see the land they love torn by violent upheaval. It is probably fair to say that the majority of South Africa's peoples, whether white or black, hope and pray that violence can be averted. They want the problem solved, not exploded.

This is not to say, of course, that they are in agreement with each other on the form of a just solution. . . . But there are, nevertheless, still men and factions and parties striving desperately to bring about change by evolutionary rather than revolutionary methods in South Africa.

Among the groups in broad opposition to Dr. Verwoerd's ruling Nationalist party, for example, there has latterly been an increased emphasis on appeals for multiracial contact and consultation. While such contact has existed on a minor scale between the fringe of liberal-minded whites and nonwhites, this accent on multiracialism is relatively new for a major, orthodox political party such as the United party.

Influence Doubtful

It would be unrealistic to overestimate the influence or extent of this new emphasis. Dr. Verwoerd has said he is opposed to multiracial consultation and went so far in parliament . . . [before the election] as to threaten to halt it if opposition parties attempted to call anything in the nature of a national multiracial political convention. . . .

Nevertheless, here are the ideas and policies of various groups which . . . [might] contribute toward a solution of South Africa's unenviable racial problem.

In the ranks of the orthodox, or parliamentary, opposition parties in South Africa, the United party is the major group, and indeed is the official opposition in parliament. This is Field Marshal Jan Smuts's old party, defeated by the Nationalists in general elections in 1948, 1953, and 1958, and now led by Sir de Villiers Graaff, a handsome and wealthy farmer-politician, and former lawyer. . . .

Over the years . . . [the United party] has pursued a "middle-road" policy, designed to avoid the racial excesses of the Nationalist party, but also designed to avoid any hint of liberalism which might alienate it even further from a conservative white electorate. . . . Sir de Villiers has spelled out his party's policy as an "ordered advance to a federation of races." He has stated clearly that the party's policy is not only to retain white leadership "for as far as can be seen in the future," but to take internal and external measures to strengthen the white group in South Africa. However, against this background, the United party is prepared to make certain concessions to nonwhites.

Common Roll Offered

As far as the Coloured (mixed-race) population of 1.5 million is concerned, the United party is prepared to restore qualified voters to the common roll with whites. Coloureds were removed from this common roll by the present government and given four whites to represent them in parliament, elected on a separate roll.

As far as South Africa's 500,000 Indian people are concerned, the United party "recognizes them as a permanent part of the population" and is prepared to negotiate with them "to determine their future political status."

The 10 million Africans the United party divides into two categories. For urbanized Africans it is prepared to revise the pass laws which currently control their movement, employment, and so forth; foster a "responsible" middle-class which could obtain freehold title to their homes; and bestow some form of representation in parliament by whites elected on a separate voters' roll.

Africans living in the rural tribal reserves of South Africa would be "guided toward a large measure of self-government" under United party policy, but the party "would insist on the retention of the authority of the central parliament." Thus, says Sir de Villiers, would emerge a federation of races, each having a share in government, and each protected through the introduction of federal elements into the constitution, "by which it is meant that each group or area is governed in a manner adjusted to its needs and state of advancement."

Sir de Villiers has also called for multiracial consultation in the form of a conference between nonwhite representatives and white experts on nonwhite affairs drawn from commerce, industry, mining, trade unions, and so forth.

Open to All Races

To the left of the United party stands the Progressive party, a splinter group which broke from the United party on the grounds that the latter's color policy was too conservative. Like the United party, the Progressives have little immediate prospect of winning enough support from a conservative white electorate to oust the present, mighty Nationalist party government.

Unlike both the Nationalist and United parties, whose membership is exclusively white, the Progressive party membership is open to all races, although only white members can sit in parliament under present law, of course.

The Progressive party would permit all citizens of a defined degree of civilization to participate in government, irrespective of race or color.

The Progressives' solution for South Africa's race problem is to introduce a dual-roll system for parliamentary elections. On the major roll, open to all races, would be voters over the age of twenty-one, and fulfilling a series of alternative financial, educational, and other qualifications. The second roll would include any literate person over the age of twenty-one who had failed to qualify for the first roll. The second roll would elect 10 per cent of the members of parliament.

This is designed to lay down civilized standards for voters on the key roll, and there would also be a bill of rights entrenching fundamental human freedoms, plus radical changes in South

Africa's constitution designed to protect any one racial group from political domination by another. If ever elected to office, a Progressive government would call a multiracial national convention to hammer out a new constitution.

One of the party's cardinal principles is that "no citizen of the Republic of South Africa shall be debarred on grounds of race, religion, language, or sex, from making the contribution to our national life of which he or she may be capable."

Liberal Party

Further to the left of the Progressive party stands author Alan Paton's Liberal party. . . . [It won no seats in the last election— Ed.] Like the Progressives, the Liberals admit all races to membership, but their problem is to win white confidence in the party's franchise policy which envisages votes for all, irrespective of race, on a common roll.

The party considers that before universal franchise can become a reality, it will be necessary to have enacted a bill of rights based on the Universal Declaration of Human Rights. It envisages major constitutional reforms, and has a civil-rights program which would involve the repeal of many existing laws which the party considers discriminatory. . . .

The only remaining opposition party functioning in the parliamentary sphere is the National Union. This is the newest party of all, and the creation of Jacob ("Japie") Daniel du Plessis Basson. Mr. Basson is a young and astute politician who broke with the ruling Nationalist party on grounds its color policy was becoming too extreme. In a way, although he was only a one-man defector from the Nationalists, his split from the government party parallels that of the Progressives from the opposition United party. . . .

On color policy he is cautious, and concentrates on modified white relations with the Coloured (mixed-race) people, whom many whites recognize as being nearer in culture to the white group than they are to Africans.

Thus his party backs direct representation in parliament by Coloureds, some form of representation in parliament for Indians, and direct representation for Indians at the provincial and municipal government level in the province of Natal, where most Indians are settled.

As far as Africans are concerned, the National Union calls for accelerated economic development of the tribal reserves, with their ultimate incorporation into a confederation of states including South Africa, South-West Africa, the neighboring Rhodesias, and the three British protectorates of Swaziland, Bechuanaland and Basutoland. For Africans in urban areas, the National Union demands relaxation of a number of restrictive measures; more consultation with Africans by white government; and representation in parliament by whites. . . .

Other Groups

There are . . . Afrikaner intellectuals who question the prime minister's direction. Recently the South African Bureau of Racial Affairs (SABRA) at the Afrikaner University of Stellenbosch has undergone an upheaval, during which criticism of the government has been freely aired.

There are also individual ministers in the progovernment Dutch Reformed Church who have urged restraint and caution upon the government. . . .

There is . . . also an extraparliamentary fringe of intellectuals which revolves around the Progressive-Liberal axis, predominantly, but not exclusively, drawn from South Africans of British stock. Thus there is the South African Institute of Race Relations and the Civil Rights League and the Black Sash women's movement, and some professors and students from the English-language universities, who in their various ways oppose government racial policy. . . .

Then there are the endeavors of certain businessmen to ease racial tension and bring influence to bear upon the government. Such financiers as Harry Oppenheimer, head of the vast Anglo American and De Beers mining empire, and Sir George Albu, chairman of the big General Mining and Finance Corporation, and John S. Schlesinger, chief of the South African Schlesinger organization, all have called in their annual reports recently for a new deal for nonwhites and for easing the tensions which have eroded foreign confidence in South Africa and caused a drastic fall-off in foreign investment. . . .

Meanwhile, barred from orthodox parliamentary activity, and since 1960 declared illegal and prohibited from any kind of political activity at all, are the African organizations.

There is the African National Congress (ANC) of ex-Chief Albert John Luthuli, and the Pan-Africanist Congress (PAC) led by Robert Mangaliso Sobukwe, serving a three-year jail term for his political activity. The ANC is prepared to cooperate in a multiracial convention to work out a new democratic constitution for South Africa. . . . The PAC, however, is much more militant, and tinged with antiwhite feeling at some levels. . . .

THE PARADOX OF SOUTH AFRICA [5]

The paradox of South Africa is that it has a Western-type parliamentary system operating for its white minority of 3 million people and a virtual police state for its nonwhite majority of over 11 million.

Seldom has this paradox been more obvious than in the crisis precipitated by the shooting on March 21 [1961], of African demonstrators at Sharpeville in the Transvaal. Continued violence has been used to break the attempts of the Africans to exert pressure on the government through demonstrations and work stoppages. Yet despite censorship and even intimidation under emergency powers, news of these events has flowed out of South Africa to an unprecedented degree. Moreover, the situation has been debated openly and fully within the country as well as outside. This is perhaps the most hopeful sign in an otherwise highly disturbing situation.

Some Whites Know Problems

Events like those at Sharpeville, and even the ruthless handling of those protesting the police action and subsequent large-scale arrests of Africans and their white and Indian supporters, are not new in South Africa. What is new is the degree of organization shown by the Africans, the widespread protests from outside and the sudden awareness by South African whites of their isolation from the rest of the world. The convergence of

[5] From "South Africa's Crisis," by Gwendolen M. Carter, professor of government at Smith College and author of The Politics of Inequality: South Africa Since 1948. Foreign Policy Bulletin. 39:141-3. Je. 1, '60. Reprinted by permission.

these three factors has produced a crisis within South Africa whose outcome will determine whether the democratic or the totalitarian features of its system will be extended.

South Africa does not lack people who are aware of the importance of developing a different basis of relationship between whites and nonwhites than that which now exists. . . .

[Especially significant] has been the growing uncertainty among both English- and Afrikaans-speaking people as to whether the country's racial policies are practicable in the light of the drastic changes sweeping throughout the African continent. Thus some Afrikaners have questioned recently whether the stringent application of apartheid to the million and a quarter Coloureds (people of mixed blood) has not alienated the one nonwhite group which could be expected to be an ally of the whites. Many businessmen have been moving cautiously but deliberately to raise nonwhite wages and give these workers a greater sense of job security. Improved African housing in the townships which ring South Africa's major cities is one of the most noticeable changes of the past two to three years. So far only a small amount of money has as yet been allocated for the economic development of the areas reserved for African occupancy whose present population continues to depend heavily on the earnings of the still larger number of Africans in the so-called white areas. Meanwhile, however, the Nationalists [have] completed . . . the legislative framework within which they maintain that the African areas (sometimes called Bantustans) may ultimately advance to self-government.

Rise of Pan-Africanists

These tentative and largely uncoordinated moves indicated concern by some South African whites for the racial issue, but they meant little to the nonwhite majority. Spasmodic riots . . . [in the summer of 1959] outside Durban and in rural districts of Natal reflected bitterness about sub-subsistence living standards and lack of adequate channels of expression. Moreover, ex-tribal Chief Albert Luthuli, a genuine moderate and for eight years head of the African National Congress (since 1912 it has been the chief mouthpiece of African aspirations), had been confined to his district in May 1959 under the Riotous Assemblies Act and banned from attending meetings for five years under the provisions of the Suppression of Communism Act. As is now apparent, the restrictions on ANC leaders, coupled with complete lack of response by the government to their appeals, opened the way for the Pan-Africanist Congress, a group of young nationalists who had fought unsuccessfully within the ANC for several years against its program of working with whites, Indians and Coloureds in the Congress movement. These embarked on April 6, 1959 on a separate effort to organize Africans to seek their own salvation.

Revolt on Passes

The demonstration at Sharpeville, the first large-scale effort by the Pan-Africanists, was against the pass system, under which Africans must carry a cumbersome document containing a wide range of permissions for such actions as living and working in urban areas. Still more than the document itself it is the arbitrary way in which the police have administered the pass regulations which has made the system the most hated badge of control over Africans. When the government temporarily relaxed pass requirements on March 26 [1960], to prevent the jails from being flooded by demonstrators, observers saw a new spirit momentarily animating urban Africans. But this spirit was quenched when the regulations were reimposed on April 6, the African National and Pan-Africanist congresses were banned for a year, and those who continued to express their opposition to government policy by staying at home were forced back to work systematically and with violence by the police, supported by the army. . . .

Impact of Outside Reactions

The concern at the Sharpeville shootings expressed by our Department of State . . . brought something of the same shock to many South Africans as had Prime Minister Harold Macmillan's quietly worded but firm speech . . . in Cape Town about the "winds of change" blowing throughout Africa. Legislatures all over the world, including the British Parliament, expressed their regret or repugnance for the violence used so openly against the Africans. . . .

South Africa's racial policy has been criticized hotly in the UN at virtually every session since the international organization came into being, but hitherto the debate and resolutions have always been in the UN General Assembly. After Sharpeville South Africa's policy was for the first time brought before the UN Security Council by the Afro-Asian group of nations as "a threat to international peace." Despite the obvious intensity of African and Asian feeling on the issue, this most complex of racial situations was analyzed with moderation within the Security Council. Impressive also was the form of the resolution the Council adopted, affirming the hope that South Africa will develop a policy based on racial equality and asking the UN secretary-general to consult with the South African government to see how such an end might be facilitated. . . .

A further spur to rethinking the long-range implications of South Africa's policy comes from the economic repercussions of the March-April events. The Johannesburg stock exchange dropped sharply after violence started and has recovered only in part since its end. South African investors have joined those from overseas in selling South African stocks. The threat of an external economic boycott, although to date more psychological than practical in its effect, is still in the background as a possibility. South Africa remains heavily dependent on outside capital, some of which comes from international agencies like the World Bank. Its businessmen, Afrikaners as well as English-speaking, have recently been the most outspoken in pressing for modifications of its racial policies to meet this very pressing African demand. It is just possible that the balance might be tilted toward a more moderate application of apartheid policies because of the need to provide a better economic atmosphere for investments.

Would such a moderate change satisfy either of the two major groups in the Union: the numerically dominant Africans or the politically dominant Afrikaners? The overwhelming bulk of the Afrikaner Nationalist community stands solidly behind its leaders. The latter know well how to play on the fears of a group which for three hundred years has safeguarded its racial integrity in the face of the far greater numbers of nonwhites, and since the 1920's has been haunted by the potential danger of being forced into "poor white-ism" through nonwhite economic competition.

Its *laager* (stockade) attitude, its implicit superiority, its sense of cohesion aided by every agency of Afrikaner life, makes the Afrikaans community one of the most self-protective in the world. Even though the economy is now strong enough to support whites at the high standards to which they are accustomed as well as to advance Africans, the sense of their conflicting interests is not allowed to die down.

Possible Changes

Already two possible changes have been called for: to increase the white population by immigration and intensify the development of the reserves so they will support a greater proportion of Africans (a policy which will need vast sums of money if the reserves are not to degenerate into rural slums); or to restrict the arbitrariness of police action toward Africans so as to make their life more stable and self-respecting in urban areas.

It is also possible, of course, that present restrictions will be maintained and even extended not only for Africans but also for others who share their aspirations for African advance. Whatever policy Afrikaner leaders agree on, their community will follow them. . . .

Afrikaner Nationalist leadership still has the power and appeal to impose its own policies on the country. What about the Africans? However much they have been crushed into submission, they have demonstrated to themselves, as well as to white South Africans, both their crucial role in the economy and their power of organization. Temporarily they are submissive under the threat of further force, with hundreds of their leaders in jail. For many, perhaps for most of them, a society in which they could have a sense of personal dignity and opportunity for economic advance would be enough. But their leaders demand a share of power so that they will have such a position by right and not by gift from the whites; so that it can be assured and not left to the exigencies of white politics. . . .

In the long run, only possession by all South Africa's people of the rights as well as responsibilities of citizenship will satisfy its African leaders, who are well aware that their unanswered claims are being granted to far less advanced Africans throughout most of the continent.

FOE OF APARTHEID: ALBERT JOHN LUTHULI [6]

Only a handful of the 2.5 million whites in the Union of South Africa have ever met a sixty-one-year-old African chief named Albert John Luthuli. He has never been asked to speak on the government radio. His picture rarely appears in the white press and then only when he is in some sort of trouble over the governing Nationalist party's policy of strict segregation, or apartheid. His winning of the Nobel Peace Prize for 1960—he learned of it . . . while cutting cane on his farm in Natal—is hardly likely to end the isolation that the Afrikaners have imposed on him. Since 1958 he has been forbidden to engage in political activity. He has been denied freedom of movement outside his native village of Groutville, in the Umvoti Mission Reserve.

Because so few of the Afrikaners—the predominant Afrikaans-speaking whites—have heard Chief Luthuli speak, there is a tendency among them to regard him as a dangerous extremist. He was among the 156 men and women of all races accused of treason in 1956. But the government was never able to formulate a satisfactory indictment against him. After the preliminary inquiry had dragged on for twelve months, Chief Luthuli and sixty others were freed, and the government later abandoned the case.

Opposed to Violence

Actually he is a moderate. Chief Luthuli hates violence and regards extreme nationalism as a greater danger than communism. He calls himself a Socialist of the British variety.

Those who have met him say their first impression was that he seemed to be a typical Zulu chief, simple, courteous, rather ponderous and platitudinous in speech. He has a square, rugged face and talks slowly, gesturing with his large hands. He speaks English with a distinct American intonation, picked up at schools run by American missionaries.

He was never antiwhite and he has never resorted to force.

As president general of the African National Congress, Chief Luthuli was intimately involved in the defiance campaign that

[6] From biographical sketch in the New York *Times.* p 22. O. 24, '61. Reprinted by permission.

swept South Africa in 1952. He helped organize demonstrations of the sit-in type against the segregation laws. Thousands of Africans invaded libraries reserved for whites, sat on railway seats "for Europeans only" and in other ways invited arrest.

The movement was well organized and led. Startled that the Africans could behave with such discipline and courage, the government crushed the movement with sharply repressive measures.

In September, 1952, Chief Luthuli was summoned to the Native Affairs Department in Pretoria and handed an ultimatum: he must resign from the African Nationalist Congress and the defiance campaign or give up his chieftainship.

Chief Luthuli replied politely that a chief, by Zulu tradition, is first the leader of his people and only secondly a government official. The government thereupon dismissed him. The tribal elders were so resentful of this that no successor to Chief Luthuli was ever named.

Summing up his political life, Chief Luthuli once wrote: "Who will deny that thirty years of my life have been spent knocking in vain, patiently, moderately and modestly at a closed and barred door?"

Chief Luthuli entered the resistance campaign an obscure country chief; he emerged a public figure. The government tried to stifle him by forbidding him to leave his home district. Chief Luthuli tried to run Congress affairs from his ramshackle house in Groutville, sending out long messages laced with biblical cadences.

The new Nobel Prize winner was a son of an African Christian missionary who went from South Africa to Rhodesia in the service of the American Congregationalist Church. He was educated at Adams College, an American missionary institution near Durban, and later taught there before being elected a tribal chief. He made a lecture tour of the United States in 1948.

Last year, in protest against the Sharpeville massacre of African demonstrators, Chief Luthuli publicly burned his passbook—hated symbol of racial segregation.

Chief Luthuli and his wife have two sons and three daughters.

A CHURCHMAN ON TRIAL [7]

The church trial of a minister of South Africa's Dutch Reformed Church on charges of heresy for having opposed racial segregation . . . [began on October 17, 1961].

The defendant is Albert S. Geyser, professor of New Testament theology at the University of Pretoria. For many years he has been an outspoken critic of racial discrimination in the church and of all racialistic ideologies. This has brought him into direct conflict both with the church and with the national policy as established by Prime Minister Hendrik F. Verwoerd and his government.

The charges against Professor Geyser were brought by three senior theological students who had been attending his lectures at the university. Details of the charges have not been made public. They are reported to cover thirteen typewritten pages derived from notes taken by the three students on Professor Geyser's lectures, personal remarks and answers to students' questions.

Colleagues of Professor Geyser both in the clergy and academic world have held that his heresy trial involves the fundamental issues of academic freedom and freedom of thought.

In addition to being accused of heresy, he also has been indicted for failure to obey a church order prohibiting criticism of church laws and decisions. Professor Geyser is to be tried by a fifteen-member synodal commission headed by the moderator of his branch of the Dutch Reformed Church, the Reverend A. J. G. Oosterhuizen.

The Dutch Reformed Church is the largest in South Africa with more than 1.3 million members drawn from the Afrikaans-speaking section of the white community as well as more than 500,000 nonwhite members who worship separately. . . .

[In November 1960] Professor Geyser took a leading part in writing and publication of a book titled *Delayed Action,* in which eleven Afrikaans-speaking theologians condemned race discrimination and called for a new outlook in South Africa's racial attitudes.

Earlier in the year he challenged his church to appoint a theological commission to examine the scriptural basis of article three

[7] From "South African Bias Foe Faces Church Heresy Trial Tuesday," by Leonard Ingalls, Johannesburg correspondent for the New York *Times.* New York *Times.* p 25. O. 22, '61. Reprinted by permission.

of its constitution which provided that only whites could be members of that branch of the church.

In his speeches Professor Geyser has attacked all racialistic ideologies, warned that these ideologies seek to use Christianity as a cloak, but are actually a direct attack on the word of God. He also has been accused of telling his students that apartheid, South Africa's official policy of racial separation, has no biblical basis. If he is found guilty of heresy, Professor Geyser could be unfrocked and dismissed from the university faculty.

THE INDIANS [8]

South African descendants of immigrants from India are groping for ways to combat color bars imposed on them and nonwhites. . . . There are 212,000 Indians living in Durban, along with 200,000 whites and about 180,000 Africans. Most of the Indians and Africans live in slum communities under conditions that have often led to clashes and bloodshed. In recent years, however, the nonwhites, who do not have the right to vote, have begun to work together for political purposes.

"We did extend the hand of friendship to the whites and they kicked it away," . . . [a] young lawyer explained. "Now the Africans have extended the hand of friendship to us and we have grabbed it."

Among the many common problems of Africans and Indians is the Group Areas Act, one of the basic laws under which South Africa's apartheid policy of racial separation is made effective. Under the Act's terms many Africans and Indians and some whites in Durban are to be forced in the next seven years to give up their homes and move elsewhere.

Those who lose their property will be compensated up to 80 per cent of its value if they are unable to dispose of it at a profit. No one objects to the slum clearance benefits of the moves but there is strong opposition to the uprooting and to being told by the government where people should live and where they should not live.

[8] From "Indians Struggle in South Africa," by Leonard Ingalls, Johannesburg correspondent for the New York *Times*. New York *Times*. p 20. My. 21, '61. Reprinted by permission.

Pay Low and Jobs Scarce

The Indian population of Durban is also troubled by low wages and unemployment. The income of the average Indian family ranges from $9 to $14 a week. About 25,000 Indians are without work. Some are supported by their relatives, but begging in the streets has become a problem.

By pooling their resources, some Indian families manage to educate their brightest children and prepare them for careers as physicians, lawyers or teachers. Yet under the government's racial policies, South Africa's major universities have been closed to most nonwhites and passports for study abroad are granted sparingly.

A TRIAL AND ITS MEANING [9]

On December 5, 1956, and some days later, 156 Africans, whites, Indians and Coloureds were arrested by the government of South Africa, accused of being members of a country-wide conspiracy inspired by international communism to overthrow the state by violence. Of the trial that . . . followed, a British observer has said: "Not since the burning of the Reichstag in Berlin in 1933—with the notable exception of the special trials at Nuremberg—has a trial attracted such international attention." Yet the trial has presented no special problem of legal correctness. . . . What does make the trial interesting and important is its political meaning, the question of its effect on the prospects for racial reconciliation in South Africa. . . .

The arrests were aimed at the leaders of the extraparliamentary opposition to South Africa's racial policies. The accused were a racially mixed and ideologically diverse group. Approximately two thirds of them (104 or 105) were Africans. Forty-four were whites and Indians (nearly the same number of each), and seven or eight were Coloureds. Of the non-Africans, a few were Communists. But the views of the rest ranged from ideological identification with the Communist world peace movement to humanitarian identification with Africans. Some of the Indians were followers of Ghandi.

[9] From "The South African Treason Trial," by Thomas G. Karis, professor of government, City College of New York, and former Foreign Service Officer in South Africa. *Political Science Quarterly.* 76:217-40. Je. '61. Reprinted by permission.

Among the Africans arrested there were only a few who had been members of the Communist party. The most important organizations represented by the accused were the African National Congress (ANC), whose leading officials were arrested, and certain bodies allied with it in the movement known as the Congress of the People. The policies of the ANC were to become the focus of the prosecution's case. Among ANC leaders who were arrested were ex-Chief Albert Luthuli, a Christian leader, . . . Professor Z. K. Matthews, academically the most distinguished African in the Union, and his son, Joe, a brilliant younger leader.

The ANC had been formed in 1912 by a tiny and conservative class of educated Africans in cooperation with tribal chiefs. Gradually it moved from a conservative African nationalism to militant nationalism and a policy of multiracial cooperation to attain its ends. In 1952, it waged a country-wide campaign of passive resistance and disobedience to the "unjust laws" of apartheid. As a result, ANC membership grew from 15,000 or 20,000 to 100,000; and about 8,500 volunteers, including some Indians, Coloureds and whites, went to jail. Rioting and violence occurred before the campaign died down by the end of the year, but, according to Professor Gwendolen Carter, the riots "were neither stimulated nor condoned by the African National Congress." The period that was to be covered by the trial's indictment—October 1, 1952, to December 13, 1956—began a few days before the first riots.

New legislation passed early in 1953 seriously increased the risks to be run in future campaigns of protest. Administrative restrictions on the activities of nonwhite and radical opponents became more and more severe during the indictment period, and police surveillance amounted to harassment. The tactics of opposition shifted from disobedience to demonstration, and multiracial cooperation grew closer. Of the campaigns of protest that were loudly proclaimed, however, many were abortive or were deflected in various ways by the government.

The climactic demonstration by the ANC and its allies was a so-called Congress of the People, held near Johannesburg on June 25-26, 1955, and attended by nearly three thousand delegates of all races. The Congress was planned by representatives of the ANC, by the South African Indian Congress, and by two organizations formed during the preceding year: the South African Congress of Democrats (largely dominated by Communist sympathizers), and the South African Coloured People's Organization. The latter two, each with only a few hundred members, supplied the white and Coloured spokes of the four-spoke wheel that symbolized the Congress of the People.

On June 26, 1955, the Congress of the People adopted a manifesto called the Freedom Charter that was to be the key document in the prosecution's case. The Charter was largely free of Communist phraseology although it displayed traces of Communist style. In the main, it rang the changes on one theme: all racial discrimination must be abolished and equal rights must be guaranteed for all. . . .

Although Communist influence was evident in the trappings and slogans at the June 1955 rally, its importance was limited. The Communists never won control of the ANC. Luthuli has always insisted that he would accept their cooperation only so long as they were not in control. Communist influence was greater among Indians than among Africans. A professed Communist, Dr. Yusuf Dadoo, who was not arrested in December 1956, was president of the South African Indian Congress. But other important Indian leaders, especially in Natal, were not Communists. . . .

There were numerous anomalies in the lists of accused and coconspirators and in the . . . [changes made in] the lists. [At the end the trial concerned twenty-eight persons.—Ed.] The most difficult to understand was the dismissal, about a year after the arrests, of Luthuli and Oliver Tambo, the ANC's second ranking official. Their dismissal seemed inexplicable when it later became clear that the ANC itself was alleged to be a party to the conspiracy, its program the essence of that conspiracy. . . .

The Trial's Political Meaning

Without imputing motives to the government, one can appreciate the logic of the trial. By it, the accused are tied up; those who might be accused are intimidated; the nature and breadth of the extraparliamentary opposition is demonstrated at home and to the world; and the demonstration is performed in accordance with the forms prescribed by a highly respected judicial system.

The government is vindicated if it wins. If it loses, it can blame defeat on the law's inadequacy and extol the meticulous standards of the judiciary. On the final decision it can base either further prosecutions or the need for new legislation.

Nevertheless, the trial has been of little value to the government in its appeal to the white electorate, of doubtful value in dealing with the nonwhite opposition, and an embarrassment abroad. The prosecution's failure to make dramatic disclosures at an early stage; the facelessness, for most whites, of the body of the accused; the tedious, complex, and protracted nature of the proceedings; and the setbacks to the prosecution—all these have made it difficult to exploit the trial politically. Whites generally have found the affair a murky business, characterized either by defense technicalities or by governmental fumbling yet probably directed at fire under the smoke. Partly because of South Africa's strict *sub judice* rules, the press has done little to clarify the trial's issues for the public.

The trial has immobilized or preoccupied many leaders of the African National Congress and diverted them from large-scale campaigns of protest. It has probably boosted the prestige of the ANC's leaders, strengthened solidarity with multiracial allies, and blurred the distinction between long-standing aspirations and Communist aims. It has hastened the emergence of younger leaders. But by partly isolating some of the leading proponents of multiracialism and gradualism, the trial has also weakened resistance to rising pressures for greater militancy, racial assertiveness, and identification with pan-Africanism. It has therefore put the ANC's leaders on the defensive on two fronts. In the longer run, however, it probably has contributed to the polarization of Afrikaner nationalism and all antigovernment Africans.

The trial has partly drained the energies of white liberals, who have accepted the burden of obligation to provide for the defense and care of the accused. The liberals include members of the Liberal party, in particular, which has competed with whites on its left in seeking African acceptance. Meanwhile, white and Indian pro-Communists, sitting day after day in the unsegregated dock of the segregated courtroom, have found the trial itself a means of closer identification with the African opposition.

Despite the prosecution's effort to stress Communist influence, hardly any foreign observers or editorial commentators have accepted the trial as a justifiably anti-Communist proceeding. It has failed to promote acceptance abroad of the claim of Dr. Hendrik Verwoerd, the present prime minister, that South Africa is the West's "best friend and most faithful ally on the African continent." Comment has mainly impugned the government's motives and sympathized with the tribulations of the accused. In a judgment that is widespread, the *Manchester Guardian* said on November 15, 1958, that the trial was "a political trial, pursued with pitiless pertinacity."

Foreign criticism has been directed at the following: the injustice of prolonged delay and uncertainty and the possibility that the trial (and successive trials) can be practically interminable; the near-impossibility of dealing fairly with individuals in a mass trial in which no single act of conspiracy nor any act of violence is alleged; the vagueness and openness to abuse of the definition of treason; the carelessness in preparing evidence and apparent arbitrariness in selecting the accused and coconspirators; the absence of any revelations about conspiracy or any convincing evidence of attempt to overthrow the government; and the severity of personal and family hardship as a result of delay and uncertainty and inadequate provision for the accused or compensation for the dismissed. No one, to the writer's knowledge, has made the charge that the trial is staged or rigged. The regularity of the trial's procedure has been highly praised but sometimes has been regarded as meaning little to the individual accused. The judges have also been praised, although sometimes in an invidious context.

The trial poses two far-reaching questions, or one question seen from two vantage points. For unenfranchised and dissatisfied nonwhites, the question is: does the breadth of the prosecution's argument leave open any extraparliamentary outlets for free speech or agitation? For whites seeking contact with these nonwhites, the question is: does the involvement in the trial of men like ex-Chief Luthuli and Professor Matthews mean that contact is possible only with Africans who are in basic agreement with official policy?

Regarding the latter question, it appears that all outlets and contacts not approved by the government are subject to being closed. Meanwhile, white anxiety about race relations has grown and with it, intellectual ferment and open-mindedness among both supporters and opponents of the government. Although their premises vary widely, these whites base their hope for eventual African consent on the preliminary step of African consultation. The trial, in showing with clarity the government's attitude toward leaders like Luthuli and Matthews, has cast a cloud on white efforts to promote consultation with such men. . . .

Conclusion

Three differing conclusions may be drawn about the trial's political importance, each of which has some validity. The Afrikaner Nationalist sees the trial as necessary. It stigmatizes subversive forces that are undermining racially separate development, the only policy that can prevent the submergence of whites by blacks. The liberal or multiracialist sees the trial as tragic. It excommunicates moderate forces with whom whites must consult if they are to bring about the conciliation and eventually win the consent that is the only hope for multiracial peace. The realist or defeatist sees the trial as symptomatic. It epitomizes the conflict of Afrikaner nationalism and African nationalism— or more ominous, white racialism and black racialism—forces that cannot be separated or reconciled. . . .

For the observer who cannot avoid the conclusion that separate development is illusory, consultation with Africans appears urgently necessary. To be effective, it can hardly exclude African leaders like Luthuli who are among the accused and alleged coconspirators (or who are among those probably destined to be accused). If the writer may claim the parliamentary privilege exercised by ministers of the South African Crown and judge a matter that is *sub judice,* Luthuli is a moderate if moderation means genuinely nonviolent in intent. But if it means willingness to accept less than fairly rapid movement toward full political equality in an integrated economy, moderation among leaders like Luthuli has been a myth for perhaps a decade.

The trial, in short, epitomizes the alienation of whites in political power from Africans who demand a share and eventually control of that power. Is it possible to foresee "graceful acquiescence" by whites? (This is the alternative to "annihilation" in

the judgment of the Roman Catholic Archbishop of Durban.)
Visiting the Union in June, 1960, C. W. de Kiewiet received the
"impression . . . that the point of no return has not yet been
reached in South Africa's internal relations." If white good will
and power and the tactic of trials can forestall movement to the
point of no return, perhaps South Africa can have a period of
grace in which new generations of whites and blacks may arise
between whom there can be accommodation.

Meanwhile, in 1961, the Special Court or the Appellate Division may finally reach a judgment for the defense. The irrele-
vance of such a judgment to the larger contest of political and
racial forces suggests the incidental nature of the trial, a dramatic
and continuing sideshow, notable for its removal of certain major
actors from the main arena.

Note: The trial came to an end suddenly on March 29, 1961,
while the defense was in the fourth week of its final argument.
Mr. Justice Rumpff announced that the three judges were unanimous in finding the twenty-eight accused not guilty. (One had
died earlier in the month.) The Court found it impossible, he
said, to conclude that the ANC had "acquired or adopted a policy
to overthrow the state by violence—that is in the sense that the
masses had to be prepared or conditioned to commit direct acts
of violence against the state." The Court would prepare a full
statement of its reasons. . . . Since the verdict was on a question
of fact and not on law, the prosecution cannot appeal—*Political
Science Quarterly.*

THE UNDERGROUND [10]

It was eleven o'clock at night when the telephone jangled in
my Johannesburg hotel room. An unfamiliar voice said: "You
came here to study apartheid; you should meet the people who
are fighting it—the underground." Then came an order to be
outside my hotel at 2 A.M.

I waited nervously outside the hotel, fingering my homburg
and stick. This had not been the first mysterious telephone call

[10] From "Underground in South Africa," by Sidney Williams, a founder of the
Canadian Society for the Advancement of Colored Peoples. *Sunday Times Magazine*
(London). p 26. My. 28, '61. Reprinted by permission of the Toronto Telegram News
Service.

I had received—nor would it be the last. A small car drew up and a well-dressed Indian held the door open for me. With him were two Africans.

We were going, I was told, to an anniversary ceremony for the seventy-one Africans who were shot down at Sharpeville. . . . It was nearly 5:30 A.M. when we reached an isolated group of houses and stopped beside a dilapidated stucco-finished cottage.

I was led down to a basement, surprisingly large and jammed with more than one hundred men and women. They were nearly all Africans in native dress, the women bare-breasted, squatting on the floor. They fell silent as soon as they saw me.

In chairs at the far end of the room a dozen white men sat, obviously in charge of the meeting. On one otherwise bare wall hung a portrait of Nikita Khrushchev draped with red flags; on another a picture of one of the leaders of the bloody Sharpeville gathering.

A tall, fair-haired white man about forty appeared to be the leader. He wore a smart, brown suit. He told me quietly, "Don't be afraid, we're not going to hurt you. We have brought you here to show that our movement is the only hope for Africa. You have been talking about communism and your hatred of it, but after seeing this meeting we believe you will change your mind and will tell your people the true facts."

Stacked Rifles

The meeting then continued in an African tongue. There were pauses to translate into other native dialects. I gathered it was a discussion of plans for unified action for some future time. When not taking part in the discussion, the tall man explained that this was a group of freedom fighters who were working to unite all parties in a common struggle for an all-black Africa.

"How," I asked, "do you propose to oust Verwoerd's government?"

He smiled, thought for a moment, then said, "I'll show you something. But first you must swear in the name of Black Africa not to reveal to a soul in Africa what you will see." . . .

At one end of the cellar was a wooden partition. The tall man leaned over, pressed a short steel rod into a small hole on the floor, and a section of the partition swung open. Inside I could

see a large room. . . . Stacked against the walls were wooden
cases made of pine. He lifted the lid on one, and inside it were
rifles. . . . In one corner stood two barrels, like rum kegs, and
in them were hand grenades. . . .

Back in the meeting room, the gathering had begun chanting.
The well-dressed Indian who had brought me said, "It's time to
go." As I left, the tall man said someone would contact me
later. . . . I tell this story not because it indicates the intent of
all black Africans, but to show the ends to which a desperate
and hopeless people can be driven.

Another Story

My second story begins at the railway station in Johannesburg.
I bought a ticket at the "nonwhites" wicket, entered a "whites
only" coach and took a seat. In a moment the conductor appeared
and with a sneer demanded, "Can't you read? You know your
kind belongs back there." He pointed along the train to the
"non-European" coaches. I said, "I'm staying here: I'm a Canadian." A dozen white passengers watched quietly, some sympa-
thetically. . . .

But the conductor ordered me off the train at the next station,
to walk back to the Coloured coaches so I wouldn't pass through
other white coaches. When I refused, the train superintendent
appeared. They talked about me in Afrikaans. Then they left.

From every side white passengers spoke up. They smiled, and
several shook hands. An Afrikaner said, "I've been trying to get
my houseboy to do this for years, but he's too frightened." An
English woman said, "If more of you would do that, you could
break apartheid." Thus I began to learn of black Africa's white
friends.

Government "Guided Tour"

When I applied for a visa to visit South Africa it was granted
on condition that I agreed to be met by government officials and
visit the places they selected. The South African High Commissioner's letter to me granting the visa explained this was necessary
"in order to enable you to obtain a complete picture of South
Africa."

At Jan Smuts Airport, outside Johannesburg, I was met by white representatives of the South African government's information bureau. I was greeted warmly and courteously. . . .

With guides and escorts provided by the government I toured the townships, or locations—the vast, sprawling native communities in which South Africa's nonwhite populations must live. . . . Some townships, in the very shadow of huge power developments, had no electricity. Children scurried everywhere, ragged, yet surprisingly clean. On every hand were pathetic evidences of pride: tiny patches of struggling lawn, flowers in windows, spotless washing hanging above the pitifully small backyards. And despite my realization that I was seeing the best, my horror grew in the knowledge that these were prisons, camps of captive and subject people. Here was obvious deprivation, malnutrition, poverty in the rags clinging to the clotheslines, but still pride in the carefully painted doors and bits of salvaged furniture. The worst slums of the Western world fall far short of conditions in many of the native townships. . . . But one has only to talk with the people to realize that the government's proposals for gradual development of the native peoples, their education and eventual local self-government, and so on, are starkly and cruelly reactionary. . . .

On "Being Black"

I was offered a fantastic salary to become a public relations man for the government to "sell" apartheid to the natives. When this offer failed, my telephone calls were monitored, attempts were twice made to "frame" me on trumped-up morality charges, and I was threatened with injury or death.

Once I walked down the street with the wife of a white lawyer. I was stopped by a policeman and threatened with a criminal charge when her husband, who was to meet us, arrived. His intervention prevented my arrest. Many times my taxis were stopped and I was threatened with a search for liquor or weapons. If I ate with a white person—except those officially approved by the government guide—it had to be done secretly. . . .

I had known discrimination at home. No one can say it does not exist in North America. But what I saw and felt in South Africa was something far more horrible. After a month, I came away frightened and disappointed. I was frightened by what obviously lies ahead: further betrayal of democracy and—if something is not done—communism.

WILL THERE BE VIOLENCE? [11]

Superficially, the situation in South Africa is quiet. It is the quietness, though, that comes when one period of struggle has ended and another has not yet begun. Two specific new factors have arisen. One is the reemergence of a Communist party organization (banned in 1950 under the Suppression of Communism Act). The other is the abandonment of the philosophy of nonviolence by many of the government's opponents. These developments are parallel symptoms of the South African *malaise*: effective legal struggle having been prohibited, the only alternative is illegal struggle.

Since the end of 1960 the Communist party of South Africa has produced, through printers in London, a publication called the *African Communist*. Latterly, it has been printing and distributing leaflets locally. On . . . [July 29, 1961] the Communist party issued a leaflet commemorating the founding of the party exactly forty years earlier. The final chapter reads:

> The Nationalist government had boasted that through the Suppression of Communism Act and other measures of persecution, in which hundreds of "listed" Communists were victimized, banned, banished and forced to resign from organizations which they had given their lives to build, they had "destroyed Communism in South Africa." It was an idle boast. . . .

New Methods

The booklet discusses with remarkable frankness the circumstances under which the Communist party dissolved itself shortly before the Suppression of Communism Act became law. This was "the culmination of a series of legalistic errors," declares the booklet. It suggests that the party should have gone underground. . . .

> Fortunately, the leaders are honest and courageous men. We have no doubt that they will recognize these errors and apply them in future campaigns. With practically every channel of legal opposition stopped

[11] From "Road to Violence in South Africa," by a special correspondent. *Observer.* p 10. S. 17, '61. Reprinted by permission.

by Dr. Verwoerd's dictatorship, it is inevitable that patriots and democrats will be compelled to an increasing extent to find new methods of
struggle which are "unconstitutional and illegal."

A Communist party leaflet adds:

> People do not get freedom served up on a plate. They have to fight
> for it. Sometimes they even have to fight with arms in their hands, as
> is now being done by the brave patriots of Algeria and Angola. . . .

It is incorrect to assume that Communists are responsible for
the present abandonment of the philosophy of nonviolence. Dr.
Verwoerd is responsible. The Communists merely endorse and
encourage the process. . . .

It is doubtful whether South Africa is the kind of country in
which armed revolt would occur. Nonwhites are known to have
tried to hoard firearms, but sabotage is probably their immediate
aim. . . . The abandonment of the policy of nonviolence by
certain nonwhite leaders does not necessarily mean that they will
start now to practice violence. But it is certainly the prelude to
violence. The restraining hand of the nonwhite leaders, who are
among the most sophisticated and reasonable nonwhites in the
whole of Africa, has been removed. . . .

Is it too late to avert violence in South Africa? Certainly,
violence can still be averted if Dr. Verwoerd is defeated *soon* at
the polls. . . .

Even Afrikaner Nationalists of course could be affected by
economic changes. The present economic setback would have to
deteriorate a lot more, however, before it undermined their
political solidarity. For one thing, the Afrikaner is at the tail end
of the country's economy: he controls less than 10 per cent of
the total economy, and possibly two thirds of the Nationalist
electorate are safely entrenched in government or semigovernment
undertakings, or they are farmers whose prices are fixed con-
veniently by control boards.

Besides, the job reservation law, which could be (and is being)
used to shift unemployment on to the nonwhites, delays the
shock even more. The Afrikaner owes his economic position,
today and tomorrow, to the props which his government has
inserted under him.

**The problem is: can economic conditions bring the Afrikaner
to his senses in time? It seems doubtful.**

If defeat at the polls is eliminated as a peaceful method of removing Dr. Verwoerd all that is left in the field of nonviolence is external pressure. Consumer and government-sponsored boycotts by the Afro-Asian states have only mildly embarrassed Dr. Verwoerd. Trade with the Afro-Asian countries has been too limited for its cancellation to upset South Africa, whose main customers are the big Western powers—and whose ever-rising gold production pays for half her total imports. . . .

A change in South Africa seems, therefore, more likely to come about from within, not from abroad; and it is more likely to come violently from the nonwhites than peacefully from the whites. By removing *all* safety valves Dr. Verwoerd is introducing textbook conditions for an explosion.

REPUBLIC HERE TO STAY [12]

When the Afrikaner Nationalist party finally vanishes from the South African scene in the not too distant future, it will leave two, and probably only two, permanent marks on the country's way of life. One will be a republican form of government. The other will be a deep-driven sense of South African nationality.

These two features, at present intended almost exclusively for Afrikaner use and advantage in a state of rigorously segregated groups, will broaden into unifying elements in one of the world's most multiracial countries. It will be no small achievement to have begun the politico-organic union of so many diverse kinds of humanity, though not quite the achievement intended by the Nationalist party now or when it embarked on its campaign for a republic in the middle of the First World War. . . .

Whatever happens there is little likelihood of a return to monarchy in South Africa. Even those who voted against the Republic did so mainly because they were anti-Nationalists rather than convinced monarchists, and also because they did not want South Africa to risk its membership of the Commonwealth. Thus the form will remain, but only as a preliminary to and container of changes which the Nationalist party has spent all its existence trying to suppress.

[12] From article by Anthony Delius, staff correspondent of a South African newspaper. *Manchester Guardian Weekly.* p 3. Je. 1, '61. Reprinted by permission.

What the Republic will almost certainly and immediately increase is that gnawing sense of South African identity. Whether you meet an African, Afrikaner, Indian, Coloured, or English-speaking South African there will sooner or later come to light in him or her an almost obsessive preoccupation with being a South African. Even the innumerable South African exiles are troubled with this South African self-consciousness. It is a deviationary southern version of the African personality. The Republic epitomizes all the crassness, greed, obsession, heroism, yearning for some or other kind of liberty, human intransigence, racial passion, and troubled respectability that have gone into the making of this irritant. Like the members of any nation destined to make some kind of mark in the world, South Africans have inserted in them by circumstances and surroundings this bit of mental grit. It is a tiresome common factor which will, as much as the single economy and the already irreversible interdependence of the various groups and races, eventually make South Africa one of the shining nonracial achievements in a naughty world.

The main conveyor of this sense of nationality among the 10.5 million Zulus, Xhosas, Vendas, Shangaans, and so on of the country is South Africa's other big nationalist movement, the African National Congress. It has had to insist upon this unifying nationality particularly because of the Afrikaner Nationalist attempt to return the African to the political helplessness of tribal factions. Now slowly, painfully, and still uncertainly this African movement is rising to take its rightful place in the politics of South Africa, after so many years of existence as the shadow cast by Afrikaner nationalism. Eventually it will become the main heir of the Republic. . . .

Watching the growing strength of the Africans in the face of all the government can do to destroy it, the Coloured people have begun to stir towards group cohesion. Because of their claim to white blood, most of the 1.5 million members of this mixed racial group have been inclined to share the antiblack prejudices of the whites, and have remained neutral at times of demonstration. Now there are signs that, as the Indians did some time ago, the Coloured leaders are moving towards an alliance with the Africans. Coloured unity, though still sketchy, is growing, and it is growing away from the old unquestioning loyalty to the whites.

This fact has disturbed those rebellious spirits in the Nationalist ranks who hoped to break down the rigid color attitudes of the majority of Afrikaners by persuading their fellows that the Coloured people were "the natural ally of the whites" in the struggle with the blacks. But Dr. Verwoerd has taken his most rigid stand yet against the incorporation of the Coloured people into "the white orbit." This, in turn, is only more likely to cause the Coloured people to look towards the Africans rather than towards the "rethinking" Afrikaners. If the Coloured people turn away altogether from the Afrikaners in the long run, this will be a considerable blow to the Afrikaners as a language and cultural group. The Coloured people are really "Brown Afrikaners," sharing the same language, churches, and, in general, history. . . .

Essentially the political tactics of 1 million English-speaking South Africans are those of a rearguard action within a rearguard action. . . . The English section showed an impressive unity when it turned out in strength to vote against the Republic, but the result revealed to them once again the futility of that unity. They are prisoners of their numbers, their wealth (they have about 75 per cent of the country's economy in their hands), and their uncertainty about what attitude to take up towards the nonwhites. This last uncertainty is reflected in the variety of political divisions among them. . . .

At the same time the English section is being steadily weakened by erosion of its top soil, its loss of brains, ability, and cultural leadership through emigration. Many of its best doctors, university men, professional people have left for Australia, Canada, the United States, and Britain. Few of the people who have gone fear a multiracial or nonracial government in South Africa. What has unnerved them is the great likelihood that an increasingly racist Afrikaner dictatorship will only be replaced by a revengefully racist African one. In the long run South Africa must reach a nonracial solution, but the emigrants cannot see it happening in their lifetime, nor do they believe they will be able to help in any way to bring it about. . . .

But there are numbers who never consider emigration—only the final settlement of what they regard as their country as much as it is the Africans' and the Afrikaners'. This is markedly the attitude of the doggedly determined inner core of liberals like Alan Paton, Peter Brown, John Lang, and Patrick Duncan. Because of men like these, and the fact that English has become the main language of protest in the country, the English section will bequeath three features to the final state of the Republic. It will have a parliamentary system, a certain tough residual liberalism, and the English language will be its medium of unifying communication.

IV. SOUTH AFRICA AND THE WORLD

EDITOR'S INTRODUCTION

Condemnation of South Africa has become habitual to the international community in recent years. Both its policies of apartheid and its handling of the mandated territory of South-West Africa have earned South Africa repeated censure within the United Nations. Opposition to apartheid within the Commonwealth of Nations caused its withdrawal from that body. New African states are especially vehement in their criticism and have invoked some measures of economic boycott against the Republic. And there is little or nothing counteracting this trend, as revealed below.

Opening the section, however, is a statement by Prime Minister H. F. Verwoerd, in which he comments broadly on the whole African scene, his own government's foreign policies, and those of the chief Western nations. The official United States view of apartheid is given by Francis T. P. Plimpton of the American Mission to the United Nations.

The decision of the Union of South Africa to leave the Commonwealth of Nations was a long-contemplated move. What the decision means both to the Commonwealth and the new Republic is explained by Gwendolen M. Carter, and an editorial from the London *Times* gives the British reaction. This is followed by notes on the British protectorates which are within or lie next to the Republic of South Africa.

The special problem of South-West Africa is dealt with in three articles: first, a general survey of the tangled legal considerations by David Johnson, professor of international and air law at the University of London; second, by Lloyd Garrison, a staff correspondent of the New York *Times*, a report on action taken by the UN General Assembly's Trusteeship Council; and third, the views of the new African states in a resolution of condemnation passed by the Conference of Independent African States in mid-1960. (The resolution also dealt with other aspects of apartheid.)

That the United States should take a firmer line is suggested by an executive of South Africa's Liberal party, Patrick Duncan, in "America Can Help." Michael Scott, the Anglican divine who has devoted his life to opposing racial segregation, next pleads for the West, and especially Britain, to lead the way in opposition to South African policies.

Albert Luthuli's speech on accepting the Nobel Peace award concludes this compilation.

THE OFFICIAL SOUTH AFRICAN VIEW [1]

A psychotic preoccupation with the rights, the liberties and the privileges of nonwhite peoples is sweeping the world—at the expense of due consideration for the rights and merits of white people. The fundamental reality being disregarded is that without white civilization nonwhites may never have known the meaning of idealism or ambition, liberty or opportunity. It seems timely, therefore, to call attention to the position of the whites, and to take note of the threat to both races inherent in any abdication by the whites of legitimate leadership.

I want to make my own position quite clear: I do not deny the nonwhite masses of the world their liberty or sovereignty; on the contrary, I endorse these concepts. But that is not the question for the moment. I am here concerned with the position of the white man in the world today. And in so doing I believe that any analysis of merit must take into account not only the merits of individuals, but the merits as well of communities and nations. Looking back through history, to whom does the credit particularly during the last centuries go for human progress, for the practical application in such infinite variety of scientific discoveries and developments? The credit goes to the white man, undoubtedly. And quite apart from his achievements in the past century and more, it is still the white man today who is at the helm of progress as we settle into the atomic era. By comparison, the numerically much stronger nonwhite nations of Africa, Asia and elsewhere have contributed little indeed since olden times to the advancement of mankind. By his

[1] From "The Price of Appeasement in Africa," statement made in a parliamentary debate, March 10, 1960, by Prime Minister H. F. Verwoerd. Text supplied by the Information Service of South Africa. Pretoria. '60. p 1-8.

initiative, intellect and organization, by his political institutions and economic vitality, the white man sets the pace of leadership and provides the trappings of civilization. . . .

In Africa nonwhite nationalism is making increasingly heavy demands under the banner of independence, demands supported morally and in practice by the Western powers. A basic assumption in this process surely must be that those who are clamoring for this should be able to grasp and maintain that which they are seeking. In other words, if it is liberty and independence they are demanding they should be capable of administering their own affairs and sustaining their own economies.

What, however, has been the case in Africa? Obviously that the new states are unable to exercise the independence granted them; that they are unable to meet their responsibilities of state without the presence of white administrators and advisers, of white technicians and entrepreneurs. The psychosis, this illusion that all the problems of black Africa would be solved merely by removing the white man from the scene has proved false.

The West, which once abetted the "whites-must-go" theory for independence, has since come to realize how important is the need for its continued aid and ministrations in Africa if the new states are not to fall prey to avid Communist aspirations or become exploited by traders and colonists from the East.

Today Western powers are bartering economic aid and technical advice in return, they hope, for the alliance of the so-called uncommitted states. What has been the result? Vigorous competition from Communist powers compels the West to raise its bidding, and as the stakes rise so neutralism becomes more and more rewarding to those who practice it. Far from winning the favor of the uncommitted new African states, the West finds itself irrevocably embroiled in a process which is stimulating and indeed entrenching the concept of neutralism. So we see emerging in Africa the enriching new posture of nonalignment: taking what you can get from both sides; playing off the lowest bidder against the highest; becoming more and more demanding, less and less loyal. And as a further outcome we see the attitude of boastful, aggressive neutralism.

To stay in the bidding for black nationalism's favors the price the West now appears willing to pay is the withdrawal of its loyalty towards the remaining white men in southern Africa.

I submit that the West is losing out in this auctioning of fidelities, that the West will fail in its objective for the very good reason that it is indulging the already discredited policy of appeasement and conciliation. . . .

Simply stated, appeasement is unwise. It does not pay. Yet in Africa today the West is following this very policy of appeasement—step-by-step capitulation to the demands of black nationalism at the inevitable expense, ultimately, of the heritage and sovereignty of the whites where they permanently settled and developed unused areas in that continent. This sacrifice of the white man of Africa is the price the West is prepared to pay in the hope that peace and quiet will prevail in Africa. I say that this is a forlorn hope. . . .

How do white men in Africa view all this competition among the bearers of gifts from East and West vying with each other for the good graces of the emergent black states? How do they view the rapid come-uppance of those black states? Here is how I see things:

There is no sign of the peaceful, cooperative, integrated and prosperous communities on which do-gooders had banked as vindication of their liberal enterprise. I believe to the contrary— that there is a far greater likelihood of chaos following upon conflicts between new states with clashing ambitions.

I see no assurance of peace in the assuaging of black national-ism, or in coming to terms with it. Such premature success of nationalism fosters the growth of individual self-interest and clique self-interest—interests which will vacillate in their affilia-tions and which could never be relied upon in the world conflict between East and West to do what the West would wish.

I see no prospect of an easing of world tensions. I foresee the United Nations organization totally disrupted by the impact of small new members ill-equipped for statesmanship and in-experienced in international negotiation—a situation from which Western nations may eventually in desperation be compelled to withdraw. . . .

I fail to comprehend how present policies in Africa supposedly will lead the black masses out of subjection. Life for them could hardly have been less pleasant under democratic white rule than it will become under the growing black dictatorship. I am certain that the political nationalism sweeping Africa has not penetrated to the masses, that these masses are not yet politically conscious or ripe for self-government and indeed that they have not the slightest interest in political ideology. . . .

I cannot see that events in Africa are strengthening or spreading the Christian gospel, despite the strong church participation in the march of liberalism. There is evidence rather of a relapse to heathenism, also that Islam is gaining over Christianity. To put it bluntly, the West is losing ground instead of gaining it in Africa.

In view of all this, what does the white man in Africa suggest? My reply, firstly, is that we eschew integration of any kind which must mean eventual submergence of white under black. Instead we suggest permanent co-existence—white states setting an example to and aiding well-founded, orderly development in neighboring black states.

Secondly, we believe that the development to full nationhood of black men should start at the beginning and proceed systematically in pace with his capabilities. Unlike other authorities in Africa we do not propose to start at the top. . . . Instead we are carefully preparing our black masses for an ever-growing share of responsibility. When the time comes for their independence, they will have become a democratically organized and democratically experienced nation, therefore their independence will not flounder upon the whim and fancy of a few power-hungry elite among them.

Thirdly, when the black states are firmly established on democratic principles alongside the white states, suitable bilateral recognition will become necessary. I have already in the past suggested a Commonwealth connection as being an example of the sort of relationship we would like to enjoy with our black neighbor states. . . .

On principle we therefore reject the policy of appeasement, the policy of soliciting by donation. What we believe in is upliftment through self-help leading to truly independent states contrasted with independent-in-name-only states. Whether a state can stand independence depends entirely on whether its citizenry is capable of and ready for independence.

THE OFFICIAL AMERICAN VIEW [2]

Apartheid is repugnant to the United States. Our deeply felt opposition is not only one of principle. It is also based on our concern for the present and future lives of millions of men, women and children who are suffering under the harsh application of apartheid. . . .

The United States also irrevocably opposes apartheid on the ground that this policy clearly violates Articles 55 and 56 of the [United Nations] Charter. These Articles pledge all members of the United Nations to promote universal respect for and observance of human rights and fundamental freedoms for all without distinction as to race, sex, language or religion. The government of South Africa has broken that pledge. However, even if there were no Charter and even if South Africa were not a member of this organization, the United States would still condemn the policy of apartheid in the strongest of terms. . . .

My government is not convinced by attempts to justify apartheid as a policy which, although obviously designed to maintain white supremacy, works to the benefit of the disenfranchised millions of nonwhite South Africans. Carried to its logical conclusion, the result of apartheid would be real partition, with the Negro and other nonwhite inhabitants in possession of their own territory and independent government and with the white South Africans gathered in their own independent enclave. However, this does not appear to be what the Republic of South Africa intends. Will the South African government ever grant full independence to those so-called Bantu states? Or does it intend to keep the nonwhite population in enclaves within its territory forever in a subordinate status and still utilize the labor of this exploited nonwhite population? There could not be a more tragic anachronism. . . .

We have no false pride when approaching the question of apartheid. As I said in a previous debate on this item,

We in the United States approach the question . . . with a certain humility; we are no strangers to many of the aspects of this problem, and we are all too aware of its complexities and difficulties. As I hope all delegates realize, our own government is dedicated to the high prin-

[2] From a statement by Francis T. P. Plimpton, United States Representative to the United Nations, in the Special Political Committee, on the question of apartheid, October 24, 1961. Press release issued by the United States Delegation to the General Assembly of the United Nations. New York. '61.

ciple that all men are created equal and should be treated equally, and our government, with the support of the vast majority of its citizens, is moving firmly and patiently toward the implementation of that high principle in all aspects of our common life throughout this country, which itself is striving to be a united nation unifying all races and all nationalities.

The history of South Africa's legislative record of the past decade is clear and irrefutable evidence, if evidence be needed, of the failure of the South African government to carry out its obligations under the United Nations Charter—and of its deliberate flouting of those obligations and of its obligations to its own peoples.

The Population Registration Act of 1950 was the first major step in a series of discriminatory, restrictive legislative acts aimed at freezing the nonwhite population of South Africa in an inferior status. The first piece of significant follow-up legislation was the Group Areas Act of 1950 which limited the legal right of the nonwhite population to live, work, and own property to certain areas specified by the South African government. There followed the humiliating pass laws which were in large part responsible for the deaths at Sharpeville. The next significant follow-up legislation was the Bantu Education Act of 1953 and its more recent corollary, the Extension of University Education Act of 1959.

Legislation enacted in 1956 and 1959 further restricted the rights of nonwhites to vote, removing them from the common rolls, and denying them a representative voice in determining their future. They are now forced to accept governmental legislation and regulations without any participation in their formulation. The Bantu Self-Government Act of 1959 repealed the last vestige of African representation in the South African parliament.

Together, these acts deny to the nonwhite population of South Africa equal opportunities with the white population— and with this denial of opportunities there follows a denial to the nonwhite peoples of equal opportunities to develop fully their potentialities of becoming useful, constructive members of the society of South Africa and the civilization of the world. . . .

Statements by high officials of the South African government in the recent electoral campaign made continuation of the policy of apartheid the main issue. The government has chosen to build its platform around the principle of continued white supremacy and opposes any attempt to restore to the nonwhite population even those basic rights which have been denied to them by the legislation described above.

The results of a continuation of the policies and practices of the past decade could very well produce a situation which would rock the entire continent of Africa. I say this because at the same time that the rights of the nonwhite population of South Africa have been diminishing, the aspirations of all Africans have rightfully been increasing.

The wave of freedom which has swept over Africa in the past decade could not be prevented from touching the minds, hearts and souls of the nonwhite South Africans—and kindling there an awareness of what should be rightfully theirs. The nonwhite population of South Africa has shown clearly that it wants the same freedoms and opportunities as the rest of the peoples of Africa. It also understands clearly that this right is being, and apparently will continue to be, denied by the government of the country in which they live—a government in which they have no voice. Throughout history where moderate efforts to bring about needed evolution have failed, or have been absent, chaos and grief have almost invariably followed. . . .

We must not despair when our efforts seem to bear no fruit. We must persevere, remembering that no man, no group of men, no government is strong enough to resist indefinitely the conscience of mankind. How and when the South African government will abandon its hateful racial policies we cannot know, but abandon them it will. And we believe, as an act of faith in our [United Nations] organization, that the work of . . . [the Special Political] Committee should and must play an important and responsible role in ending a bleak and unhappy chapter in the history of the African continent and in opening up a brighter future for all Africans.

SOUTH AFRICA AND THE COMMONWEALTH [3]

South Africa . . . left the Commonwealth, not because the other members refused to continue its membership after it became

[3] From article by Gwendolen M. Carter, professor of government at Smith College and author of *The Politics of Inequality: South Africa Since 1948. Foreign Policy Bulletin.* 40:113-14. Ap. 15, '61.

a republic, but because its prime minister, Dr. Hendrik F. Verwoerd, was unwilling to remain in an association which expressed such strong repugnance for the Union's policy of racial
discrimination known as apartheid.

By leaving the decision to South Africa the Commonwealth
adhered to its historic practice of keeping its door open to all
former members of the British Empire. But by taking a firm
stand against apartheid the Commonwealth remained true to the
logic of its own multiracial character and to the standards of
human self-respect on which it is based.

South Africa's decision to leave the Commonwealth has important consequences both for itself and for that unique association. It is true that most of the material advantages commonly
associated with participation in the Commonwealth—membership in the sterling bloc, the lower tariffs on certain goods which
result from imperial preference, easier entry for its citizens into
other Commonwealth countries, particularly Britain, Canada,
Australia and New Zealand, and easier acquisition of citizenship
—will doubtless still be open to South Africa, although in some
cases special arrangements will have to be made. But the retention of these advantages will not be sufficient to compensate for
the psychological effects of the break. Since World War II the
Commonwealth has been the only international association of
which South Africa was a member where its racial policy has not
been subject to constant and bitter attacks. Now its isolation is
still further intensified. . . .

Afrikaners, whose ancestors came to South Africa some three
centuries ago, differ basically from other European groups on the
African continent in that they have no outside country . . . to
which they could look for support and even refuge in case of
difficulties. In order to reduce the tension under which most
white South Africans live because of being outnumbered 4 to 1
by nonwhites in the Union and 60 to 1 on the continent, they
need to establish the same bonds of mutual interest and support
with the peoples of the West as other white residents overseas
have with their countries of origin. The South Africans, however, by increasing obvious discrimination against nonwhites instead of attempting to eliminate it, as other Western peoples,

however hesitantly, are trying to do, have reduced even those ties of friendship which most informed Western observers, aware of the complexities of the situation, had once had with them.

Impact on Afrikaner

At the moment it is natural to feel great sympathy for the more than 1 million English-speaking whites in South Africa. Many of them, particularly in Natal, have a strong loyalty to the Commonwealth, and indeed to the Crown, which South Africa would have eliminated in any case from its internal and external policy when it became a republic on May 31, 1961. Yet it is perhaps on the ruling Afrikaners that the impact of the break with the Commonwealth will have greatest effect. One of the most significant questions today is whether South Africa's withdrawal from the Commonwealth will mean an intensification of the Afrikaner *laager* (armed camp) attitude of self-protection against the world, including their fellow South Africans of English descent—or whether, as some Afrikaners have long predicted, it might strengthen a common sense of identity between white South Africans, the more so because the pressures of African nationalism are increasingly difficult to insulate within their country.

But what of the Commonwealth? South Africa's withdrawal and the strength of the feeling against apartheid which prompted this decision have given the Commonwealth, perhaps temporarily but maybe permanently, a positive quality which it otherwise lacked. Before World War II, the Commonwealth was overwhelmingly British in character. Since 1945, its remarkable expansion to include India, Pakistan, Ceylon, Malaya, Ghana, and most recently Nigeria and Cyprus, has made it a genuinely multiracial association, the only one in the world in which leaders from countries of such different racial and cultural backgrounds have met at frequent intervals to exchange views frankly, and in enviable privacy, about matters of common and international concern.

Strength of Commonwealth

The Commonwealth's emphasis on noninterference in internal affairs developed naturally from the fact that its members, except for Britain, were originally colonies which moved to independence by eliminating Britain's rule. Its strength has been the sense of mutual interest, most dramatically expressed when its overseas members, of their own free will, entered World War II in support of Britain and proved its staunchest allies in the dark days after the fall of France and before our entrance into the war.

In the postwar period it has been abundantly clear that the new unifying purpose felt by almost all Commonwealth members was the struggle for popular self-determination and against racial discrimination. To this struggle the British government has been giving intelligent and forceful leadership in Africa, where it still has important commitments, in an attempt to safeguard the interests of white resident minorities as well as to provide essential training for the leaders of African majorities. It was Mr. Macmillan who solemnly warned the South African parliament in February 1960 that the "winds of change" were blowing throughout Africa and, indeed, throughout the world. The Commonwealth's stand on South Africa represents a landmark in its long and remarkable development: an assertion by implication of full friendship and partnership on the basis of equality between nations whose populations together number one quarter of the world's total people despite their different races, colors, backgrounds and stages of development. In a world beset by strains, none of them more subject to exploitation than those arising from racial intolerance, no action could be more healthy or more promising.

A REPRESENTATIVE BRITISH VIEW [4]

The South African government leaves the Commonwealth having already, thanks to those who have held power for the last thirteen years, lost the friendship and respect not only of British countries but of the world. The only questions being asked outside the Union are how long will this narrow racial tyranny last and how, if at all, can the transition to a happier, more just and stable state be made without bloodshed. That is not how Dr. Verwoerd and his colleagues see it, and . . . their case should fairly be put first. They base themselves on one fundamental

[4] From "Bankrupt," editorial. *The Times* (London). p 13. My. 31, '61. © The Times Publishing Company Limited, 1961. All Rights Reserved. Reprinted, by permission, from *The Times* for May 31, 1961.

belief which their supporters express in these words, "We know how to handle the Kaffir."

Everything that has happened since Mr. Macmillan made his famous speech in the houses of parliament at Cape Town about the "winds of change" has confirmed them in this belief. They point in an exultant spirit of "We told you so" to British, French, and Belgian scuttlings from African colonies, to mounting tension in areas north of the Limpopo, where the white writ still runs, and to gross deviations from the most elementary principles of democracy in some areas which have come under African rule. The contrast with conditions in the Union is, they maintain, all to their advantage. "Troublemakers" and "agitators" are under lock and key and, in consequence, the economy of a prosperous and expanding community has not been upset, as wishfully thinking observers hoped that it would be, by the prelude in the last few days to the setting up of a republic.

Why, they continue, should there be any hard feelings about this constitutional change? No ill will to Britain is implied. Loyalists in Natal, the eastern province, and elsewhere would be better employed in settling down as good South Africans, shoulder to shoulder with their Afrikaans-speaking fellow citizens, than in waving the Union Jack. There is work ahead for all, white, Coloured, black, and even, presumably, for the Indians— unless the Nationalist creed still requires its faithful to regard Indian South Africans as aliens. A complex of more or less independent states is to be built up within the frontiers of the Union, allowing for men and women of each color to develop separately and to the fullest extent that is ordained for them by God.

Such is the doctrine that, in varying degrees of coherence and courtesy, the defenders of apartheid preach. They affirm that it is a Christian doctrine which gives no unfair advantage to any section of society and that its merits have been hidden or distorted by wicked journalists and other men of ill will, in and outside the Union. They have been repeating this plea ever since Malan defeated Smuts in 1948 and the present trend of events began, slowly at first but with increasing tempo, to gather momentum. As a last resort they accuse their opponents of sour grapes, of never having forgiven the South African electorate for throwing over the greatest Boer that, in the eyes of many English people, had ever appeared in public life.

This whole case of the Nationalist government is based on a series of fallacies. The British are not vindictive or given to looking back into the past. Their quarrel with the Nationalists is not that Smuts was put out of office but that no one with a contemporary idea in his head has been put in his place. The Nationalists in 1948 stopped the clock. Confronted with the twin tasks of finally healing the wounds that were still felt, though with increasing mildness, by Boer and Briton and of grappling with race relations, they were overtaken by spiritual and intellectual paralysis. . . . They lapsed into sour parochialism. At first this was not resisted either by the Dutch Reformed Church, from which the Afrikaners draw so much strength, or by the leaders of thought at such centers of true learning as Stellenbosch. It is significant that recently some predikants and professors—men whose words carry weight among their fellows—have been showing themselves less and less in sympathy with Dr. Verwoerd and his well-disciplined inner circle of rulers.

Doubts in the Union spring from the same two causes that are effective elsewhere in the world among those who are aware of what is happening on the South African stage. The first is that the pretense of a divinely imposed difference between people of this or that color commands no serious respect. It is an anachronistic make-belief and its hollowness must become more and more obvious as the years go on. The second doubt—it is now accepted even in the Union as almost a certainty—derives from the patently impractical nature of the Bantustan concept. The carving up of an integrated industrial society into artificial parts based on color distinction cannot be done. To say that there is no life left in the corpse of apartheid is to pay its champions an undeserved compliment. It never had a life to lose. A stuffed dummy substitute for a real contemporary policy is stretched across the public life of the Union with its sawdust gushing out for all to see.

Until this is swept off into the wings and South Africa again has a government that thinks in terms of the age in which its subjects, whatever their color, are living, there can be no future for the Union, except a gathering uncertainty that must influence the well-being of the nation to the very core. Dictatorship may seek to put off the hour of reckoning by more restrictions on personal liberty, freedom of the press, and the other rights of democratic peoples. It is not by such negations of constructive statesmanship that the Union will be saved from the evil plight in which she now finds herself. The most that outside observers can say today is this: All power to the majority of South Africans in saving themselves from the consequences of the long reign of bankrupt policies.

THE BRITISH PROTECTORATES [5]

In common with other British dependencies, the High Commission Territories of Basutoland, Swaziland, and the Bechuanaland Protectorate have made considerable constitutional progress in the last few years and it has been officially confirmed that the British government wishes them to develop into self-governing political units, able to stand on their own feet both economically and politically.

Until recently the High Commission Territories were the responsibility of the Commonwealth Relations Office, and the U.K. high commissioner in South Africa held the additional position of high commissioner for these Territories. However, with South Africa's withdrawal from the Commonwealth in May 1961, a new situation arose. To meet it, new arrangements were brought into effect and on 1 December 1961 the Colonial Office assumed the responsibility for the Territories. For the time being Sir John Maud, who is now Britain's ambassador to the Republic of South Africa, will continue to fulfill the dual role of high commissioner for the Territories.

This somewhat anomalous position reveals the serious problem with which the British government is faced in these three Commonwealth outposts. On the one hand there is the wish and commitment to develop them as viable entities on a nonracial basis, in line with Commonwealth principles and policy—an objective which is, in any case, made difficult by the familiar circumstances prevailing in underdeveloped countries which have few resources of their own. On the other hand there is, in the case of the High Commission Territories, the additional com-

[5] From "Recent Developments in the High Commission Territories." *World Today.* 18:17-23. Ja. '62. Reprinted by permission.

plicating factor that these three Territories, in many aspects of their life, are almost wholly dependent upon South Africa. Geographically they are practically enclosed by the Republic: Basutoland has no other outside borders, while Bechuanaland's border with the Rhodesias is not of a nature to facilitate international communication. Probably the only effective international boundary is that of Swaziland and Mozambique. . . .

Politically, development in the High Commission Territories has been distinct from the Republic of South Africa, and no question of incorporation arises today. Economically, however, they have been a virtual extension of South Africa. They share South Africa's currency system, make use of South Africa's communications, and have a customs union with South Africa in terms of which goods can move freely in and out of the Territories and the South African customs pay over to the Territories a proportion of the revenue they collect. An even stronger link has been the fact that South Africa has offered virtually the only source of employment for inhabitants of the Territories—particularly in the South African gold mines. It has been estimated that on an average 150,000 Basutos are to be found in the Republic in gainful employment at any particular time. Workers from Bechuanaland and Swaziland also migrate to the Republic to seek work in considerable numbers.

The mineworkers are recruited as contract labor, but other work-seekers are likely to suffer disabilities in the Republic, where they are regarded as "foreign natives." The South African prime minister, Dr. H. F. Verwoerd, was reported as saying at the National party congress recently that relations with the High Commission Territories would now have to be put on the basis of relations with a foreign state.

Interference with this flow of labor would probably not be in the interests either of South Africa or of the High Commission Territories, and it will be convenient if some arrangement can be made between the British and South African governments for its continuation. The same applies to the customs union. On the other hand, it is obviously necessary that the economies of the three Territories should be developed as rapidly as possible in order to keep pace with the constitutional development which has already begun to take place. Before considering plans for economic development, however, it may be useful to note briefly the main features of political development in the three Territories.

Basutoland, with a population of 641,674, of which approximately 2,000 are non-African, is politically the furthest advanced of the Territories. A new constitution was introduced in 1960 which provides for a legislative council (the Basutoland national council) composed of eighty members, one half of whom are elected from members of district councils. The district councillors are elected on a common roll franchise. Seventy-six of the eighty members of the legislative council are African, and fourteen of the nonelected members are nominated by the paramount chief. Others sit *ex officio* as chiefs and four senior officials of the administration are also members. There is also an executive council which consists of these four officials (including the resident commissioner) and four unofficial members of the Basutoland national council. The paramount chief retains important executive functions; ultimate legislative authority is vested in the high commissioner. Recently, the Basutoland national council resolved to ask the high commissioner to review the constitution with a view to introducing a greater measure of self-government.

The Bechuanaland Protectorate has a population of 292,755, of which about 3,000 are non-African. Under a new constitution introduced in 1961, elections for a legislative council were held in May. The council has ten African and ten European elected members and one Asian member, in addition to nominated members and officials. Seretse Khama, former chief of the Bamangwato, received the greatest number of votes in the voting for African seats. Two Africans, of whom Seretse Khama is one, also sit in the ten-member executive council. Elections to the legislative council are on a pyramidal system and direct elections have not yet been envisaged. The first meeting of the legislative council took place on 20 June 1961.

Swaziland, with a population of 264,300, of which approximately 10,000 are non-African, is at present the least advanced of the three Territories from a constitutional standpoint. The resident commissioner, who is responsible to the high commissioner, is advised by a European advisory council of ten elected members, and the (African) Swaziland national council. The paramount chief of the Swazi nation, Sobhuza II, has considerable authority and powers over his African people.

A new constitution is now planned for Swaziland, and in November 1961 the appointment of Sir Charles Arden Clarke, former governor-general of Ghana, as constitutional adviser was announced by the secretary of state for Commonwealth relations. The Swaziland Progressive party, which is a political party representing progressive African opinion in the Territory, asked Professor Denis Cowen, the South African constitutional lawyer who advised the Basutos on their constitution, to draft proposals for submission on their behalf to the constitutional committee. It is understood that both Sir Charles and Professor Cowen have now completed their reports.

It was confirmed in the House of Commons on 23 November that it is the policy of the British government that Swaziland shall move forward to a new constitution on an entirely nonracial basis. A number of racially discriminatory laws have been repealed by proclamation, and further steps of this kind are being considered.

In the economic sphere, progress in the Territories has been rather uneven. A mission was appointed by the high commissioner in mid-1959, in consultation with the International Bank for Reconstruction and Development, to investigate possibilities of economic development. It was headed by Professor Chandler Morse of Cornell University and reported in July 1960, advocating an acceleration and expansion of the existing development program.

Of the three Territories, Swaziland is the best equipped with natural resources; Basutoland and Bechuanaland are chiefly pastoral economies. The export of cattle to South Africa is the mainstay of the Bechuanaland economy: the value of such exports in 1959 was £3.5 million. The Morse mission recommended water conservation schemes to overcome the serious lack of water in most parts of the Territory and also the development of the livestock industry. It stressed the need for the scientific application of new techniques in marketing, transport, etc., and for improved communications. Foot-and-mouth disease is a serious problem for Bechuanaland's cattle industry. A potential source of future revenue could be mineral deposits, and geological surveys are being conducted by several mining companies.

Basutoland exports wool and other primary products—again mainly to the Republic of South Africa. The value of its exports in 1959 was £1.5 million. Soil conservation and better land use were recommended by the Morse mission, as in the case of Bechuanaland, as well as improved communications and a program of agricultural research. There has been a useful development of agricultural cooperative societies in Basutoland and the Morse mission recommended that this movement should be encouraged.

Swaziland has a good climate and generally adequate rainfall. Afforestation is undertaken on a commercial basis by the Colonial Development Corporation (CDC), and the Usutu Pulp Company, jointly owned by the CDC and Courtaulds Limited, produces and exports unbleached pulp to markets in the United Kingdom. Swaziland also has important mineral deposits. Asbestos has been worked at the Havelock mine for some years, and a project is now under way for the development of the considerable iron ore deposits at Ngwenya, some thirteen miles northwest of Mbabane, the capital. The Swaziland Iron Ore Development Company Limited has signed a contract with Japanese iron and steel companies for the sale of 12 million long tons of high-grade ore from Ngwenya over the next ten years. The value of this contract is in the region of £40 million, and the company is a joint project of the Anglo American Corporation of South Africa and Guest, Keen and Nettlefold Ltd. The CDC is also to participate in the equity of the company.

The opening up of these iron-ore deposits has been made possible by the decision to build a new railway through Swaziland linking it with the Portuguese territory of Mozambique. An announcement from the Commonwealth Relations Office in September stated that the Portuguese government had agreed to extend the existing railway from Goba to the Mozambique-Swaziland border, thus providing a through rail link to the port of Lourenço Marques. It is hoped that the line will be open for traffic in 1964. The major share of the necessary capital for the Swaziland portion of the railway—which is planned to run from Ngwenya southeast to Siphofaneni and then northeast to the Portuguese border—will be provided by the CDC and the Anglo American Corporation. The cost is estimated at £8 million. The railway is to be managed by a Swaziland railway board, to be established by proclamation.

In addition to timber and mining industry, there is considerable cultivation of such crops as cotton, rice, tobacco, and vegetables, often on a cash basis, and irrigation schemes are being put into effect. The new rail link and the development of industry which it will make possible should open up important new avenues of employment not only to Africans in Swaziland but possibly also to those from the other Territories, and the economic prospects for Swaziland would appear very bright.

From 1945 to 1961 the United Kingdom advanced nearly £10.5 million to the High Commission Territories from colonial development and welfare funds. The under-secretary of state for Commonwealth relations announced on . . . [July 6, 1961] that authority was being given to the high commissioner to incur development expenditure up to £1.2 million in the period ending 31 March 1963, over and above that already authorized under the Colonial Development and Welfare Acts. This means that the high commissioner will dispose of nearly £6 million from 1961 to March 1963 for existing and new schemes. The possibility of finance from international organizations, and particularly the International Development Association, is also being investigated.

All this economic progress is most welcome, but it is clear that much more will be needed, particularly in Basutoland and Bechuanaland, before the High Commission Territories can be said to have a fair chance of survival as independent units. In particular, educational facilities in all three Territories need to be rapidly improved and expanded, and technical training schemes instituted—questions on which the Morse mission was definite in its recommendations.

The crux of the problem, however, is the need to arrive at a satisfactory basis of coexistence with South Africa, with the Territories preserving their own independence and nonracial structure of society.

SOUTH-WEST AFRICA [6]

The status of South-West Africa, a sparsely populated territory, largely desert and as big as France and the United Kingdom

[6] From "The South West African Issue in International Law," by David Johnson, professor of international and air law at the University of London. *Optima.* 11:118-24. S. '61. Reprinted by permission of *Optima,* a quarterly review published by Anglo American Corporation of South Africa.

combined, has been the subject of dispute for fifteen years. In one form or another this matter has already been referred three times to the International Court of Justice, and will return to it again now that Ethiopia and Liberia have decided to initiate proceedings against South Africa, requesting the court to declare that South Africa "has the duty to cease forthwith the practice of apartheid in the territory of South-West Africa."

Since 1915, when this former German colony surrendered to South African forces, the territory has been administered by the South African government as an integral part of the country. The territory is divided into a Police Zone and the Northern Tribal Area. In the Police Zone, which covers about 66 per cent of the whole area of some 318,000 square miles, live most of the 70,000 white people. The majority speak Afrikaans; the German-speaking group is the second largest, and the English-speaking by far the smallest group. Roughly a third of the nonwhite population of about 450,000 also live in the Zone, largely in reserves. Administration of the Northern Tribal Area is by the traditional system of indirect rule through the chiefs. The tribes include the Hereros, Ovambos, Hottentots or Namas, and Damaras, and there are also some primitive Bushmen.

The most populated area, containing the capital, Windhoek, is the central plateau, which is two to six thousand feet above sea level and lies between two deserts, the Namib on the Atlantic coast and the Kalahari to the east. The main industries are mining, fishing and sheep and cattle farming. Diamonds are mined from coastal deposits north of Oranjemund, which are the world's largest individual source of gem stones; copper, lead and zinc, the other leading minerals, are mined in the north. The dry southern area is a major supplier of "Persian" lamb pelts from the Karakul sheep.

At the Versailles Conference in 1919 the South African government pressed for the incorporation of the territory into the Union of South Africa. It was, however, the proclaimed policy of the principal Allied and associated powers (Great Britain, the United States of America, France, Italy and Japan) that territories outside Europe surrendered by Germany and Turkey after the First World War should not be annexed as colonies, as they previously would have been, but should be governed instead as "mandated territories" by mandatory powers under the auspices of the League of Nations. In accordance with this policy, the mandate over South-West Africa was conferred upon "His Britannic Majesty to be exercised on his behalf by the Union of South Africa." There has been some suggestion that, upon South Africa's becoming a republic, she is bound, under both international law and Commonwealth constitutional law, to surrender the mandate for South-West Africa to the government of the United Kingdom. There seems to be little force in this suggestion. This is not to say, however, that the principal Allied and associated powers, the parties to whom Germany originally surrendered South-West Africa under the Treaty of Versailles, may not still have some ultimate rights in, and some ultimate responsibilities for, the territory.

Article 22 of the Covenant of the League of Nations provided in general terms that "to those colonies and territories which as a consequence of the late war have ceased to be under the sovereignty of the states which formerly governed them and which are inhabited by peoples not yet able to stand by themselves under the strenuous conditions of the modern world, there should be applied the principle that the well-being and development of such peoples form a sacred trust of civilization and that securities for the performance of this trust should be embodied in this covenant." Further, under the League of Nations, mandated territories were classified as follows. First, there were Class A mandates, e.g., Lebanon, Syria, Palestine, Trans-Jordan and Iraq. . . . All these territories have become independent, Iraq as long ago as 1932. Secondly, there were Class B mandates—Togoland (French and British), Cameroons (French and British), Ruanda-Urundi (Belgian) and Tanganyika (British). Here, too, the process of attaining independence is virtually complete, although this goal was not provided for in Article 22. All that was required of the mandatory powers was that they should administer the territories in question "under conditions which will guarantee freedom of conscience and religion," and avoid abuses such as the slave trade, the arms traffic and the liquor traffic. Mandatory powers were also forbidden to establish fortifications or military or naval bases, to give military training to the natives for other than police purposes and the defense of territory, and were obliged to secure equal opportunities for the trade and commerce of other members of the League of Nations. Thirdly, there were Class C mandates, consisting of South-West Africa, and also a number of islands or island groups in the Pacific. In the case of these mandates, Article 22 enacted that ". . . (they) can be best administered under the laws of the mandatory as integral portions of its territory, subject to the safeguards above mentioned in the interests of the indigenous population." These safeguards were the same as those applicable to the Class B mandates. Finally, Article 22 of the covenant provided that the League organ responsible for the supervision of the mandates should be the council, assisted by a permanent commission, which came to be known as the Permanent Mandates Commission. . . .

[In the particular case of South-West Africa, the terms of its mandate were further elaborated in the mandate itself which provided that if disputes arose between the mandatory and another League member regarding the applications of the mandate, such dispute should be submitted to the Permanent Court of International Justice.—Ed.]

The mandatory powers were required to submit annual reports to the League of Nations, upon which they could be questioned either in the commission or in the council. Provision was made in 1923 for written petitions to be sent to the commission, through the respective administering mandatory powers by inhabitants of the mandated territories dissatisfied with certain aspects of administration. So far as South-West Africa was concerned, however, this right was not exercised during the time of the League of Nations. . . .

From 1934 onwards, the Union of South Africa began to press for the complete incorporation of South-West Africa. No decision was taken, however, and the international status of the territory remained, at least formally, unchanged until the League of Nations and the Permanent Court of International Justice ceased to exist in 1946. . . .

[Subsequently the United Nations and the International Court of Justice have been deemed to be successors of the League and the older court, although the technical legal issues involved are not so easily summarized. Instead of the mandate system, the very different trusteeship system for the former mandates, as well as for territories taken from states defeated in World War II, came into effect. South Africa did not follow the example of other states and conclude with the United Nations a trusteeship agreement for its former mandated territory. Rather, it proclaimed its aim of incorporating South-West Africa into the Union of South Africa. On this matter the UN General Assembly asked the International Court of Justice for advice. Although such advisory opinions are not binding, the court's opinion of 1950 was to the effect that the original mandate had not lapsed, that South Africa could not unilaterally modify the international status of South-West Africa, but that the United Nations must give its consent also. Tangled legal questions have been argued since both within the United Nations and between South Africa and the United Nations.

In 1960 matters came to a head when Ethiopia and Liberia took the initiative of taking to the International Court another problem—this time alleging that the Union government's apartheid policy as a whole constituted a violation of the mandate. This matter is still under adjudication. However, despite the legal problems involved, most observers fear that the political issues will, as they have since World War II, determine the outcome of the struggle between South Africa's aims and those of the international community.—Ed.]

A CALL FOR ELECTIONS IN SOUTH-WEST AFRICA [7]

The General Assembly's Trusteeship Committee overwhelmingly approved . . . [on December 13, 1961] an African-Asian resolution calling for general elections leading to the independence of South-West Africa. The resolution goes considerably further than a measure adopted last year by the committee. Last year a United Nations study group was set up to seek to visit the territory and report on conditions there.

South Africa, which administers South-West Africa under a League of Nations mandate, was present during the balloting, but did not vote on the resolution. Despite "certain qualms," the United States voted in favor of the resolution, as did eighty-five other nations. Portugal cast the only negative vote. Britain, France, Belgium and Spain abstained.

[7] From "U.N. Unit Asks Vote in South-West Africa," by Lloyd Garrison, staff correspondent, New York *Times*. New York *Times*. p 1+. D. 14, '61. Reprinted by permission.

The resolution calls for a special seven-man mission to visit South-West Africa by May 1 [1962], with the task of achieving the following objectives in consultation with South Africa:

1. Evacuation of all South African military forces with the exception of civilian police.

2. Release of all political prisoners "without the distinction of party or race."

3. Repeal of all laws maintaining apartheid, or racial separation.

4. Preparation of general elections to the legislative assembly, to be held as soon as possible under United Nations control.

5. Guidance for the government on preparing the territory for full independence after the elections have been held.

6. The resolution also urged South Africa to allow African exiles to return to South-West Africa without fear of detention or imprisonment.

The United States' "qualms" centered on the resolution's unreserved approval of the report of last year's study group. The group was barred by South Africa from entering South-West Africa and most of its information was based on evidence taken from exiles and other secondary sources.

Although the United States voted for the resolution as a whole, the United States seemed to prefer a more moderate Swedish proposal, which was defeated. The main feature of the Swedish proposal was a clause taking into account a South African offer to invite three past General Assembly presidents to visit South-West Africa and make an on-the-scene report, which South Africa would publish in full. . . .

During the debate, sponsors of the African-Asian resolution said they harbored no doubts that South Africa would reject all of their recommendations. In that event they said, they would ask for a special session of the Security Council and seek direct United Nations intervention.

AFRICAN STATES PROTEST [8]

On South-West Africa

The Conference of Independent African States meeting at Addis Ababa, having considered the question of the territory of South-West Africa; . . . concludes that the international obligations of the Union of South Africa concerning the territory . . . should be submitted to the International Court of Justice for adjudication in contentious proceeding. . . .

On Economic Measures Against South Africa

Having learned with indignation of the death of many African political leaders in the prisons of the Union of South Africa thus adding to the already long list of victims of the shameful policy of racial discrimination;

Recalling Resolution No. 1375 (XIV) adopted by the United Nations General Assembly condemning the policy of apartheid and racial discrimination practiced by the government of the Union of South Africa;

Recalling further the Security Council's Resolution of April 1, 1960 recognizing the existence of a situation in South Africa which, if continued, might endanger international peace and security;

Reaffirming the declaration of Bandung and the resolutions adopted at Accra and Monrovia regarding this shameful policy;

Noting that, despite world opinion and the resolutions adopted by the United Nations, the government of the Union of South Africa still persists in its evil policy of apartheid and racial discrimination; [the Conference of Independent African States]

(1) Desires to pay homage to all victims of the shameful policy of apartheid and racial discrimination; (2) decides to assist the victims of racial discrimination and furnish them with all the means necessary to attain their political objectives of liberty and democracy; (3) calls upon member states to sever diplomatic relations or refrain from establishing diplomatic

[8] From statement of the Conference of Independent African States, Addis Ababa, June 14-26, 1960, as reprinted in South Africa and World Opinion, by Peter Calvocoressi. Oxford University Press. London. p 64-6. '61.

relations as the case may be, to close African ports to all vessels flying the South African flag, to enact legislation prohibiting their ships from entering South African ports, to boycott all South African goods, to refuse landing and passage facilities to all aircraft belonging to the government and companies registered under the laws of the Union of South Africa, and to prohibit all South African aircraft from flying over the air space of the independent African states; (4) invites the Arab states to approach all petroleum companies with a view to preventing Arab oil from being sold to the Union of South Africa and recommends that the African states refuse any concession to any company which continues to sell petroleum to the Union of South Africa; (5) invites the independent African states which are members of the British Commonwealth to take all possible steps to secure the exclusion of the Union of South Africa from the British Commonwealth; (6) recommends that appropriate measures be taken by the United Nations in accordance with Article 41 of the Charter; (7) appeals to world public opinion to persevere in the effort to put an end to the terrible situation caused by apartheid and racial discrimination; and (8) decides to instruct the Informal Permanent Machinery to take all steps necessary to secure that effect shall be given to the above recommendations and to furnish full information on cases of racial discrimination in the Union of South Africa so that the outside world may be correctly informed about such practices.

AMERICA CAN HELP [9]

The real touchstone of American intentions in Africa lies in South Africa. If the United States truly wants to march at the head, then it must stand alongside Africa in the last and toughest struggle—the struggle against apartheid. Unfortunately it is just in this area that there are signs that President Kennedy has not yet been able to impose his thinking on the policy of the United States. This ambiguity, this lack of purpose, may be due to the $300 million invested by American businessmen in South Africa. Or it may be the result of purely military

[9] From "South Africa: America Can Help," by Patrick Duncan, a member of the national executive of the Liberal Party in South Africa. *New Republic*. 145:19-21. Jl. 3, '61. Reprinted by permission.

and strategic considerations. Whatever the cause, the following facts appall African nationalists and South African Liberals:

1. The United States Embassy in South Africa is still "For Whites Only." True, the color line was once broken, two ambassadors ago, when an American journalist, Mr. William Gordon, was asked to a cocktail party. But the experiment was not repeated and no mixed dinner parties have yet been held. I do not blame the ambassador or his staff. They serve the United States well and do not wish to make a radical departure from precedent, which could provoke an incident with Dr. Verwoerd's racialist government in South Africa. If a change is to come it must come from Washington. The ambassador has extraterritoriality, and could legally entertain anyone he pleases, despite South African racial laws. A consul has no such protection, yet the last Soviet consul-general entertained nonracially and diplomatic relations were ended by the Union on this account. As the independent African states look to South Africa and compare the Soviet record there with the American, can they be blamed for questioning American sincerity?

2. Dr. Verwoerd's government makes great play of its anti-communism. Sometimes even American officials are taken in by this. On May 2, Dr. Angus Tresidder, in charge of all United States information activities in South Africa, speaking to an audience composed mainly of Afrikaner nationalists, said, "America regards South Africa as the country which must lead the rest of the continent. . . . South Africa is . . . known for the steadfast manner in which it opposes communism." But since Dr. Verwoerd is known throughout the world, and particularly in Africa, as a ruler who suppresses Africans, when he opposes communism, Africans all over the continent think better of communism. And when Dr. Tresidder speaks appreciatively of Dr. Verwoerd, Africans all over Africa think worse of America. Dr. Tresidder said in the same speech that "America and South Africa must stand closely together against the Communist danger."

3. The United States is cooperating closely with Dr. Verwoerd in the military and strategic field. This cooperation cannot fail to damage American policy in Africa. For the South African armed forces are not normal armed forces: the highest sources have told us that they are primarily designed to suppress the nonwhite South Africans. . . .

There are not wanting military minds in Washington who cannot think further than the recently-built missile tracking station in South Africa. With the new accent on space there is a real danger that such voices may prevail and that America may forge real and lasting links with apartheid.

In 1961 the United States voted for a watered-down resolution at the United Nations on the South-West African issue. It is possible to make a good case for the vote. The issue was whether action should be called for, or not, and it is possible to argue that *at this moment* sanctions are not feasible. But the decision to vote against action reminded Africa of all the ambiguous votes of the United States in 1960—the support of Portugal (the worst African colonizer), against Liberia for a seat in the Security Council, the abstention on the resolution calling for a UN-sponsored plebiscite on Algeria, and the abstention on the key resolution authorizing the Committee on South-West Africa to investigate the territory on the spot. Worst of all, the United States abstained on a resolution which called for a speedy end to colonialism, without mentioning a target date. [Subsequently the United States voted to censure the Portugese regime in Angola. The United States also took a strong stand against apartheid— see "The Official American View," in this section, above.—Ed.]

As a liberal South African, I hope, of course, that President Kennedy will be strong enough to impose his ideas and remove these offenses. But more than the mere removing of offenses is called for. The Communist bloc is pouring money into South Africa. Much of the finance for the abortive end-of-May strike was brought to South Africa by a well-known African nationalist leader who had visited Peking and Moscow. This support is given to stimulate real opposition to apartheid and to help pro-Communists into positions of leadership in the liberation struggle.

Since under an increasingly Nazi-like government normal methods of open political opposition will become decreasingly possible, the West must either play a part in supporting un-conventional opposition or leave the field to the Communists. And to leave this field would mean that once again, as in Algeria, the West would be forced onto the side of the status quo, because the side of progress and freedom would have had Communist help.

What Can Be Done?

Is it possible to see any sort of strategy at this stage? I think so. The first area where a successful breakthrough against apartheid could be made is South-West Africa. The Union's title to the mandate over this former German colony is probably bad: a lawsuit now before the International Court of Justice is expected to give a decision on this point in a few months.

Let the General Assembly of the United Nations assume its rights and revoke the mandate, in accordance with the advisory opinion of the same court that the rights and duties of the old League of Nations toward South-West Africa have devolved on the General Assembly. Let the United States decide no longer to hold back, but to lead in the matter. It will be easier than ever now that South Africa has left the British Commonwealth. The revocation of the mandate will, of course, need teeth, just as other United Nations operations in Africa have needed teeth. This the United States must realize when it makes its decision on South-West Africa.

The revocation of the mandate would be a shock which the apartheid government would be unlikely to survive. But if it were to survive the shock a liberated South-West Africa could be the jumping-off ground for successful political action to end and replace apartheid. Still, the question of revocation of the Union's mandate is for the future, though not the remote future. For the present there is something that needs doing urgently and can be done.

Neglect of its mandatory obligation to uplift the people means that the Union has educated very few Africans in South-West Africa. Fewer than ten have university degrees. Those with successfully-completed high school careers amount to a few dozen only. What is needed is the establishment of an adult education college for South-West Africa—and perhaps for other refugees from apartheid—something on the lines of Tanganyika's Kivukoni College. . . . At Kivukoni no formal education certificates are required or granted. But a general background in political and administrative knowledge will be given men and women who have shown they can play a part in public life. Such a college is desperately needed for South-West Africa and could possibly be established in Bechuanaland or Tanganyika by one or more of the great American foundations. Such a college might do much to avoid a Congo-like breakdown in the future in South-West Africa.

A high-ranking American official once said to me that if the United States were to use its influence to end the apartheid regime it could do so. I believe he is right. And if he is right, then something of the responsibility for the continued existence of the world's worst racialist government since Hitler must rest on those in America who, having such power, refuse or neglect to use it. Quite simply, those inside South Africa who could help are afraid. I submit that for America to be neutral in the struggle against apartheid is to neutralize American policy in all Africa. And if the new Kennedy line were to fail in Africa it must fail in the whole underdeveloped world. Such a disaster need not happen.

THE WEST MUST HELP [10]

It would be presumptuous for anyone living outside South Africa to advise the oppressed there to keep their struggle for justice nonviolent. No one could claim that under the circumstances that prevail in South Africa today, he or she would be capable of taking positive nonviolent action, or even of following the example of the justly honored Albert Luthuli and remaining nonviolent in face of the provocation and aggression to which the nonwhite people are being subjected. [See "Foe of Apartheid: Albert John Luthuli," in Section III, above, and "A Nobel Peace Award Speech," below.]

But there are disturbing remarks to be heard these days. They run along the lines: "Well, the whole show will obviously blow up one day and the whites have certainly asked for what is coming to them."

Holocaust of Hatred

Is it so sure what the outcome of a resort to violence would be? Certainly, it could be disastrous for the white population and for the industries they own. But the white people also have a virtual monopoly of the weapons of mass destruction.

[10] From "Violence or Non-Violence in South Africa?" by the Reverend Michael Scott, an Anglican priest who actively opposed apartheid while serving in South Africa. *Observer.* p 10. N. 19, '61. Reprinted by permission.

Sometimes one fears that the "showdown" mentality has become so irrational on the part of some of the rulers of South Africa that they would almost welcome a fight. Few who know South Africa can doubt that those who hold power would not stop at mass extermination of Coloured, Indian and African alike, if it seemed to be a choice between that and a violently enforced reversal of the present position of dominance with the nonwhites replacing the whites.

Large-scale violence in South Africa, whoever starts it, would let loose a holocaust of hatred and destruction the like of which has not yet been seen anywhere in Africa or Asia. Intervention in some form, by East or West, or by both, would be almost inevitable. That is why the South African situation is menacing to the peace of the whole world.

There are many cogent reasons why the South African situation should not be allowed to drift into violence. But is there a way by which the processes of civilization could intervene effectively before it is too late? Is it beyond the ability of the Western powers to initiate a process of carefully thought out pressures and sanctions in this dire situation of the white man's making?

We certainly cannot afford to pursue any longer a policy of shilly-shallying. If we do, the West will one day find itself blamed by the rest of the world for a hideous massacre that will bring discredit on the whole character and integrity of Western civilization itself.

A beginning could be made by taking a firm line over the South-West African mandate. The subjection of the people of this territory to the South African government on doubtful legal grounds has now been debated in the General Assembly of the United Nations every year for the last fifteen years. But the mistreatment of Africans in this territory, particularly those who make any gesture of political protest, continues unchecked. Hideous stories could be related of what is occurring there today. This is the issue on which international pressure on South Africa should first be concentrated.

Positive Measures

The sanctions that should be applied against South Africa for noncompliance with the requests of the General Assembly could be of many kinds. The most effective would be the economic pressure that could be brought to bear by a determined attitude in Washington and London. But this should be balanced by positive measures to make the British protectorates, that exist on the Republic's border and in its midst, examples of political and economic progress. If this were done through international agencies, it would add to the local prestige of the United Nations —which, as in the Congo, may be the only usable agency when the ultimate crisis comes.

Time is fast running out. Britain is the country best placed to give a lead to the world. Unless sufficient pressure from outside is brought to bear on the South African government, a disaster will surely occur there and it is impossible to foresee how far its consequences may spread.

A NOBEL PEACE AWARD SPEECH [11]

The Nobel Peace award that has brought me here has for me a threefold significance. On the one hand it is a tribute to my humble contribution to efforts by democrats on both sides of the color line to find a peaceful solution to the race problem. This contribution is not in any way unique. To remain neutral in a situation where the laws of the land virtually criticized God for having created men of color was the sort of thing I could not, as a Christian, tolerate.

On the other hand the award is a democratic declaration of solidarity with those who fight to widen the area of liberty in my part of the world. As such, it is the sort of gesture which gives me and millions who think as I do tremendous encouragement.

There are still people in the world today who regard South Africa's race problem as a simple clash between black and white. Our government has carefully projected this image of the problem before the eyes of the world. This has had two effects. It has confused the real issues at stake in the race crisis. It has given some form of force to the government's contention that the race problem is a domestic matter for South Africa. This, in turn,

[11] Excerpts from speech delivered in Oslo, December 11, 1961, by ex-Chief Albert John Luthuli, Nobel Peace Prize winner for 1960. Text from the New York *Times*. p 12. D. 12, '61.

has tended to narrow down the area over which our case could be better understood in the world.

From yet another angle, it is a welcome recognition of the role played by the African people during the last fifty years to establish, peacefully, a society in which merit and not race would fix the position of the individual in the life of the nation.

Award Seen for All Africa

This award could not be for me alone, nor for just South Africa, but for Africa as a whole. Africa presently is most deeply torn with strife and most bitterly stricken with racial conflict. Ours is a continent in revolution against oppression. And peace and revolution make uneasy bedfellows.

There can be no peace until the forces of oppression are overthrown. Our continent has been carved up by the great powers. In these times there has been no peace. There could be no brotherhood between men. But now, the revolutionary stirrings of our continent are setting the past aside. Our people everywhere from north to south of the continent are reclaiming their land, their right to participate in government, their dignity as men, their nationhood.

Thus, in the turmoil of revolution, the basis for peace and brotherhood in Africa is being restored by the resurrection of national sovereignty and independence, of equality and the dignity of man.

It should not be difficult for you here in Europe to appreciate this. Your age of revolution, stretching across all the years from the eighteenth century to our own, encompassed some of the bloodiest civil wars in all history. By comparison, the African revolution has swept across three quarters of the continent in less than a decade, its final completion is within sight of our own generation. Again, by comparison with Europe, our African revolution to our credit is proving to be orderly, quick and comparatively bloodless.

Our goal is a united Africa in which the standards of life and liberty are constantly expanding, in which the ancient legacy of illiteracy and disease is swept aside, in which the dignity of man is rescued from beneath the heels of colonialism which have trampled it. . . .

Goal Held Way to Peace

There is a paradox in the fact that Africa qualifies for such an award in its age of turmoil and revolution. How great is the paradox and how much greater the honor that an award in support of peace and the brotherhood of man should come to one who is a citizen of a country where the brotherhood of man is an illegal doctrine.

Outlawed, banned, censured, proscribed and prohibited; where to work, talk or campaign for the realization in fact and deed of the brotherhood of man is hazardous, punished with banishment or confinement without trial or imprisonment; where effective democratic channels to peaceful settlement of the race problem have never existed these three hundred years, and where white minority power rests on the most heavily armed and equipped military machine in Africa.

This is South Africa.

Even here, where white rule seems determined not to change its mind for the better, the spirit of Africa's militant struggle for liberty, equality and independence asserts itself. I, together with thousands of my countrymen, have in the course of struggle for these ideals been harassed and imprisoned, but we are not deterred in our quest for a new age in which we shall live in peace and in brotherhood.

South Africa Assailed

It is not necessary for me to speak at length about South Africa. It is a museum piece in our time, a hangover from the dark past of mankind, a relic of an age which everywhere else is dead or dying.

Here the cult of race superiority and of white supremacy is worshipped like a god. The ghost of slavery lingers on to this day in the form of forced labor that goes on in what are called farm prisons.

It is fair to say that even in present-day conditions, Christian missions have been in the vanguard in initiating social services provided for us. Our progress in this field has been in spite of, and not mainly because of, the government. In this the church in South Africa—though belatedly—seems to be awakening to a broader mission of the church, in its ministry among us.

I, as a Christian, have always felt that there is one thing above all about "apartheid" or "separate development" that is unforgivable. It seems utterly indifferent to the suffering of individual persons, who lose their land, their homes, their jobs, in the pursuit of what is surely the most terrible dream in the world.

This terrible dream is not held on to by a crackpot group on the fringe of society. It is the deliberate policy of a government, supported actively by a large part of the white population, and tolerated passively by an overwhelming white majority, but now fortunately rejected by an encouraging white minority who have thrown in their lot with nonwhites who are overwhelmingly opposed to so-called separate development. . . .

Freedom Wanted

The true patriots of South Africa, for whom I speak, will be satisfied with nothing less than the fullest democratic rights.

In government we will not be satisfied with anything less than direct individual adult suffrage and the right to stand for and be elected to all organs of government.

In economic matters we will be satisfied with nothing less than equality of opportunity in every sphere, and the enjoyment by all of those heritages which form the resources of the country which up to now have been appropriated on a racial "whites only" basis.

In culture we will be satisfied with nothing less than the opening of all doors of learning in nonsegregatory institutions on the sole criterion of ability.

In the social sphere we will be satisfied with nothing less than the abolition of all racial bars.

We do not demand these things for people of African descent alone. We demand them for all South Africans, white and black. . . .

Africa's Age

This is Africa's age—the dawn of her fulfillment, yes, the moment when she must grapple with destiny to reach the summits of sublimity saying, ours was a fight for noble values and worthy ends, and not for lands and the enslavement of man.

Still licking the scars of past wrongs perpetrated on her, could she not be magnanimous and practice no revenge? Her hand of friendship scornfully rejected, her pleas for justice and fair play spurned, should she not nonetheless seek to turn enmity into amity?

Though robbed of her lands, her independence and opportunities to become—this, oddly enough, often in the name of civilization and even Christianity—should she not see her destiny as being that of making a distinctive contribution to human progress and human relationships with a peculiar new Africa flavor enriched by the diversity of cultures she enjoys, thus building on the summits of present human achievement an edifice that would be one of the finest tributes to genius of man?

In a strife-torn world, tottering on the brink of complete destruction by man-made nuclear weapons, a free and independent Africa is in the making, in answer to the injunction and challenge of history: "Arise and shine, for thy light is come."

Acting in concert with other nations, she is man's last hope for a mediator between the East and West, and is qualified to demand of the great powers to "turn the swords into ploughshares" because two thirds of mankind is hungry and illiterate.

Africa's qualification for this noble task is incontestable, for her own fight has never been and is not now a fight for conquest of land, for accumulation of wealth or domination of peoples, but for the recognition and preservation of the rights of man and the establishment of a truly free world.

BIBLIOGRAPHY

An asterisk (*) preceding a reference indicates that the article or a part of it has been reprinted in this book.

BOOKS AND PAMPHLETS

Adam, T. R. Government and politics in Africa, south of the Sahara. Random House. New York. '59.

Ballinger, R. B. South-West Africa. South African Institute of Race Relations. Johannesburg. '61.

Brookes, E. H. South Africa in a changing world. Oxford University Press. New York. '54.

Brookes, E. H. and Macaulay, J. B. Civil liberty in South Africa. Oxford University Press. New York. '59.

*Callan, Edward. Albert John Luthuli and the South African race conflict. Western Michigan University Press. Kalamazoo. '62.
   Reprinted in this book: Map of South Africa, by Eugene Kirchherr. p 8.

*Calvocoressi, Peter. South Africa and world opinion. Oxford University Press (issued under the auspices of the Institute of Race Relations). New York. '61.
   Reprinted in this book: "Statement of the Conference of Independent African States." p 64-6.

Carter, G. M. Politics of inequality: South Africa since 1948. Praeger. New York. '58.

Carter, G. M. and Brown, W. O. Transition in Africa; studies in political adaptation. Boston University Press. Boston. '58.

Cowen, D. V. Foundations of freedom, with special reference to southern Africa. Oxford University Press. New York. '61.

De Beer, Z. J. Multi-racial South Africa; the reconciliation of forces. Oxford University Press (issued under the auspices of the Institute of Race Relations). New York. '61.

De Kiewiet, C. W. Anatomy of South African misery. Oxford University Press. London. '56.

Horrell, Muriel, comp. Days of crisis in South Africa (events up to 15th of May 1960). mimeo. South African Institute of Race Relations. Johannesburg. '60.

Horrell, Muriel. Economic development of the "reserves": the extent to which the Tomlinson commission's recommendations are being implemented. mimeo. South African Institute of Race Relations. Johannesburg. '59.

Horrell, Muriel. "Pass laws." South African Institute of Race Relations. mimeo. Johannesburg. '60.

Horrell, Muriel. Race classification in South Africa—its effects on human beings. mimeo. South African Institute of Race Relations. Johannesburg. '59.

Horrell, Muriel. Racialism and the trade unions. South African Institute of Race Relations. Johannesburg. '59.

*International Commission of Jurists. South Africa and the rule of law. The Commission. Geneva. '60.
    Also available from American Fund for Free Jurists, Inc. 36 W. 44th St. New York 36.

Italiaander, Rolf. New leaders of Africa; tr. from the German by James McGovern. Prentice-Hall. Englewood Cliffs, N.J. '61.

Kuper, Leo. Passive resistance in South Africa. Yale University Press. New Haven, Conn. '57.

Luthuli, A. J. Let my people go. McGraw. New York. '62.

Marquard, Leopold. Peoples and policies of South Africa. 2d ed. Oxford University Press. New York. '60.

Melady, T. P. Profiles of African leaders. Macmillan. New York. '61.

Millin, S. G. People of South Africa. Knopf. New York. '54.

Molteno, D. B. Betrayal of "natives' representation." South African Institute of Race Relations. Johannesburg. '59.

Molteno, D. B. Towards a democratic South Africa. South African Institute of Race Relations. Johannesburg. '59.

Paton, Alan. Hope for South Africa. Praeger. New York. '59.

Pienaar, S. and Sampson, Anthony. South Africa: two views of separate development. Oxford University Press. New York. '60.

*Plimpton, F. T. P. Statement on the question of apartheid. U.S. Delegation to the General Assembly of the United Nations. New York. O. 24, '61.
    Press Release

Reeves, Ambrose. Shooting at Sharpeville, with a foreword by A. J. Luthuli. Gollancz. London. '60.

Robertson, H. M. South Africa: economic and political aspects. Duke University Press. Durham, N.C. '57.

Roux, E. R. Time longer than rope; a history of the black man's struggle for freedom in South Africa. Gollancz. London. '48.

Segal, Ronald. Political Africa: a who's who of personalities and parties. Praeger. New York. '61.

Spooner, F. P. South African predicament: the economics of apartheid. Praeger. '61.

United States. Senate. Committee on Foreign Relations. United States in the United Nations, 1960—a turning point; supplementary report to the Committee on Foreign Relations, by Senator Wayne Morse, February 1961. 87th Congress, 1st session. Supt. of Docs. Washington 25, D.C. '61.

*Verwoerd, H. F. Price of appeasement in Africa. South African Information Service. Pretoria. p 1-8. Mr. 10, '60.

PERIODICALS

Africa Report (Africa Special Report). 2:1+. O. '57. "Separate development" in South Africa. E. S. Munger.

Africa Report (Africa Special Report). 5:5+. F. '60. South-West Africa —the people, the problems, the prospects. Adam Clymer.

*Africa Report (Africa Special Report). 5:3-4+. D. '60. Apartheid in a hostile world. Vernon McKay.

Africa South. 4:30-41. Jl.-S. '60. African and Indian in Durban. Fatima Meer.

Africa South. 5:44-8. Ap.-Je. '61. Crisis in the Dutch Reformed churches. James Oglethorpe.

African Affairs. 59:301-10. O. '60. Impressions of my visit to South Africa; with discussion. Rebecca West.

African Affairs. 59:56-65. Ja. '61. Policy of apartheid. B. P. Erasmus.

African Affairs. 59:77-108. Ja. '61. Constitution-making for a democracy. D. V. Cowen.

*Atlantic Monthly. 205:14+. Je. '60. Atlantic report: South Africa.

Atlantic Monthly. 207:58-61. Je. '61. Isolation of South Africa. Dan Jacobson.

Atlantic Monthly. 209:61-4. Mr. '62. If I were prime minister. A. J. Luthuli.

*Baltimore Sun. p 12. Je. 20, '61. Uneasy republic. Leo Marquard.

*Banker. 111:405-9. Je. '61. South Africa faces its crisis.

Christian Century. 79:148-9. Ja. 31, '62. South Africa. A. W. Blaxall.

*Christian Science Monitor. p 9. Ag. 20, '59. South Africa—after 50 years. John Hughes.

*Christian Science Monitor. sec 2, p 9. Jl. 21, '61. South Africa searches. John Hughes.

Commercial Opinion (South Africa). 38:6-8. Jl. '60. Proposals to ease race tension: memorandum by five organisations to the prime minister.

Commercial Opinion (South Africa). 38:15. S. '60. Business leaders state their views: Towards human and political emancipation, by R. N. Harvey; The red light, by E. V. E. Homes.

Commonweal. 74:292-3. Je. 16, '61. Republic of South Africa.

Contemporary Review. 197:280-2. My. '60. Diamonds in South Africa. Peter Holz.

Contemporary Review. 198:487-9+. S. '60. Fifty years of the Union. L. E. Neame.

Contemporary Review. 199:76-9. F. '61. Apartheid: the South African treason trial and human rights. Norman Bentwich.

Current Biography. 23:21-3. F. '62. Albert John Luthuli.

Current History. 40:104-9. F. '61. Apartheid in South Africa: history of apartheid and its implications. J. L. Barkon.

Current History. 41:225-31. O. '61. Winds of change in southern Africa. C. R. Lovell.

Economist. 194:506-7. F. 6, '60. Frankness between friends.

Economist. 194:1088. Mr. 19, '60. Dr. Verwoerd replies.

Economist. 195:274. Ap. 16, '60. Investment reappraisal: money out of Africa.

Economist. 195:1193. Je. 18, '60. Legalizing tryanny.

Economist. 196:1096+. S. 17, '60. Irrelevant referendum.

Economist. 197:217-18. O. 15, '60. White Africans; thicker than blood.

Economist. 197:251-2. O. 15, '60. South Africa's choice.

Economist. 197:866. N. 26, '60. Dr. Verwoerd's hopes.

Economist. 197:1305. D. 24, '60. Republic of granite.

Economist. 198:937. Mr. 11, '61. South African boycott: no success.

Economist. 198:1160-4+. Mr. 25, '61. After South Africa.

Economist. 199:905-8. My. 27, '61. One sane country.

Economist. 199:1146. Je. 10, '61. Mr. Oppenheimer speaks out.

Economist. 200:640-2. Ag. 12, '61. Dr. Verwoerd's desert island.

*Economist. 201:358. O. 28, '61. Dr. Verwoerd's mandate.

Foreign Affairs. 39:670-82. Jl. '61. South African prospect: thoughts on an alternative race policy. Sir de Villiers Graaff.

*Foreign Policy Bulletin. 39:141-3. Je. 1, '60. South Africa's crisis. G. W. Carter.

Foreign Policy Bulletin. 40:61-2. Ja. 1, '61. New look at South Africa. C. W. de Kiewiet.

*Foreign Policy Bulletin. 40:113-14. Ap. 15, '61. South Africa and the Commonwealth. G. M. Carter.

*Fortune. 61:152-65. My. '60. Harry Oppenheimer's industrial Africa.

Fortune. 65:47+. Ja. '62. Cost of apartheid.

Harper's Magazine. 224:42-5. Mr. '62. Why I left South Africa. Dennis Craig.

International Organization. 13:82-3. Winter '59; 14:124-6. Winter '60. Policies of apartheid of the government of the Union of South Africa.

Journal of Politics. 22:682-97. N. '60. Apartheid and politics in South Africa. E. A. Tiryakian.

*Life. 48:32-41+. Ap. 11, '60. South Africa torn by fury; with historical account. Gene Farmer.

*Manchester Guardian Weekly. p 3. Je. 1, '61. Republic here to stay. Anthony Delius.

Manufacturer (South Africa). 10:28-30. Jl. '60. Our difficulties are matters of social and economic discontent. H. F. Oppenheimer.

New Commonwealth. 38:695-8. N. '60. New hope for South Africa. Jan Steytler.

New Commonwealth. 39:361-4. Je. '61. South Africa outside the Commonwealth. A. S. Kruger.

New Leader. p 44+. O. 2, '61. Guided tour of apartheid. J. K. Sale.

*New Republic. 144:17-18. F. 20, '61. Why apartheid will not work. H. F. Oppenheimer.

*New Republic. 144:18-19. F. 20, '61. What chance have the moderates? Adam Clymer.

New Republic. 144:7. Mr. 27, '61. South Africa, gone with the wind. Denis Healey.

*New Republic. 145:19-21. Jl. 3, '61. South Africa. America can help. Patrick Duncan.

New Statesman. 59:207. F. 13, '60. What Macmillan really said. James Fairbairn.

New Statesman. 59:473-4. Ap. 2, '60. African tragedy. James Fairbairn.

New Statesman. 60:74-5. Jl. 16, '60. Feudal tradition survives.

New Statesman. 60:263. Ag. 27, '60. Sex is colour-blind.

New Statesman. 60:410. S. 24, '60. New Boer republic.

*New York Times. p 20. My. 21, '61. Indians struggle in South Africa. Leonard Ingalls.

New York Times. p 31. Je. 4, '61. Whites ask talks for South Africa. Leonard Ingalls.

*New York Times. p 8. O. 12, '61. Address before the United Nations General Assembly, October 11, 1961. E. H. Louw.

New York Times. p 11. O. 20, '61. Verwoerd party bolsters hold with 10 per cent gain in votes. Leonard Ingalls.

*New York Times. p 25. O. 22, '61. South African bias foe faces church heresy trial Tuesday. Leonard Ingalls.

*New York Times. p 22. O. 24, '61. Foe of apartheid: Albert John Luthuli.

*New York Times. p 12. D. 12, '61. Speech delivered in Oslo, December 11, 1961. A. J. Luthuli.

*New York Times. p 1+. D. 14, '61. U.N. unit asks vote in South-West Africa. Lloyd Garrison.

*New York Times. p 17. Ja. 24, '62. First Bantu state established within South Africa; advertisement of the Information Service of South Africa.

*New York Times Magazine. p 28-9+. My. 22, '60. From veld to city: the Bantu drama. Anthony Sampson.

New York Times Magazine. p 8+. S. 4, '60. White dilemma in black Africa. Alan Paton.

New York Times Magazine. p 9+. My. 28, '61. Republic for which South Africa stands. Alan Paton.

*New York Times Magazine. p 42+. S. 24, '61. Human meaning of apartheid. Nathaniel Nakasa.

New Yorker. 37:164-5. Ap. 22, '61. Letter from London. Mollie Panter-Downes.

Newsweek. 57:45-6. Mr. 27, '61. Commonwealth: all alone.

Newsweek. 58:38. S. 4, '61. South African Reich.

*Observer. p 10. S. 17, '61. Road to violence in South Africa.

*Observer. p 10. N. 19, '61. Violence or non-violence in South Africa? Michael Scott.

*Optima. 11:118-24. S. '61. South West African issue in international law. David Johnson.

*Political Science Quarterly. 76:217-40. Je. '61. South African treason trial. T. G. Karis.

Progressive. 25:31-4. Mr. '61. Africa's southwest hell. Sheridan Griswold.

Reporter. 22:8. Ap. 28, '60. Africans and Afrikaners.

Reporter. 23:19-22. S. 1, '60. At the cape of desperate hope. Anthony Delius.

Round Table. 50:134-9. Mr. '60. Academic apartheid; segregation of South African universities.

Round Table. 50:223-33. Je. '60. South African tragedy; a study of the failure of apartheid.

Round Table. 51:3-6. D. '60. Republic of South Africa: its relation to the Commonwealth.

Saturday Review. 43:20-1. N. 26, '60. Escape from apartheid. Norman Phillips.

*Scotsman. p 13. My. 26, '60. Africans' revolt against pass laws. George Clay.
    Same with title Pass system: how it operates. Africa Special Report. 5:7+. My. '60.

Senior Scholastic. 78:17. Ap. 5, '61. Commonwealth shift.

Spectator. 204:650+. My. 6, '60. Schizoid state. Nicholas Mosley.

Spectator. 205:237. Ag. 12, '60. White hope. Kenneth Mackenzie.

Sunday Times Magazine (London). p 26. My. 28, '61. Underground in South Africa. Sidney Williams.

*Time. 75:18-19. Ap. 4, '60. Sharpeville massacre.

*Times (London). p 13. My. 31, '61. Bankrupt.

Twentieth Century. 168:58-65. Jl. '60. Anatomy of Afrikaner nationalism. Michael Picardie.

U.S. News & World Report. 48:84+. Ap. 18, '60. Official statement on race troubles in Africa; text of official statement made by the government of the Union of South Africa.

*U.S. News & World Report. 48:138-9. Je. 20, '60. Apartheid: is it really race discrimination? W. C. du Plessis.

U.S. News & World Report. 49:108-9. N. 7, '60. From troubled South Africa, a candid talk to the West. E. H. Louw.

U.S. News & World Report. 50:49-51. Je. 5, '61. Another race conflict: showdown in South Africa.

U.S. News & World Report. 51:86-8. D. 18, '61. Diplomat's advice: keep South Africa as a friend. P. K. Crowe.

United States Department of State Bulletin. 45:638-42. O. 16, '61. Southern Africa in transition. G. M. Williams.

Vital Speeches of the Day. 26:290-4. Mr. 1, '60. Commonwealth independence and interdependence ["The winds of change"]; address to the South African parliament, Cape Town, February 3, 1960. Harold Macmillan.

Washington Post. p A10. Ag. 14, '61. Exodus begins in South Africa. Stanley Uys.

World Politics. 11:44-67. O. '58. Conflict of nationalisms in South Africa. C. R. Nixon.

World Today. 16:181-94. My. '60. Statutory background of apartheid; a chronological survey of South African legislation. Margaret Cornell.

World Today. 16:233-42. Je. '60. Crisis in South Africa. Colin Legum.

World Today. 17:135-42. Ap. '61. South Africa's withdrawal and what it may mean.

*World Today. 17:538-46. D. '61. South Africa faces the future.

*World Today. 18:17-23. Ja. '62. Recent developments in the High Commission Territories.

Worldview. 3:3-7. Jl.-Ag. '60. Economics of apartheid. Sean Boud.